WILD ABOUT RACING

MY LOTUS YEARS WITH CLARK AND CHAPMAN

To John Remembering Jim Clark

DEREK WILD

DEDICATION

To my Dad – Bernard Eugene Wild (17/05/09 - 23/06/78) – who started my love of motor racing.

Top: *Dad (centre) emerging virtually unscathed from his workplace in Smithfield after the last V2 of the Second World War went straight through the factory, but didn't explode.* © Sports and General, London.

Bottom two photos: *Dad around the time when he first started taking me to races.*

CONTENTS

ACKNOWLEDGEMENTS

I would like to thank my wife, Shirley – without her help, none of this would have been possible.

Likewise, to Darren and Kevin of BHP Publishing for taking the book on. It means a lot to finally get it out there. BHP's in-house designer, Lucy Arbuthnott, has done an excellent job.

All photos were taken by me during my tenure at Lotus unless otherwise credited.

I am very grateful to Peter Darley, The Jim Clark Trust (JCT), and Classic Team Lotus (CTL), for permission to use some of their excellent images.

To check race results, I used Anthony Pritchard's book, *Lotus – All The Cars*, extensively.

Louis Stanley's *Grand Prix* books were a great help to jog my memory!

First published June 2024

© Derek Wild

ISBN: 978-1-7385085-1-8

Author: Derek Wild
Editors: Darren Banks & Kevin Guthrie
Designer: Lucy Arbuthnott
Media/PR: Charlie Scordecchia-Wilson
Print Manager: Derek Fulton

Front cover image: © Derek Wild archive/Auto International
Rear cover image: © Derek Wild archive

Printer: Halcyon Print Management
Publisher: BHP Publishing (Fife, Scotland)

Designed and printed in the UK

FOREWORD

This book is a collection of Derek's memories and anecdotes from his time at Lotus, as well as his insights into the personalities and technologies that shaped the golden era of motorsport. It is a rare and valuable account of what it was like to work with some of the legends of the sport, such as Colin Chapman, Jim Clark, Graham Hill and Jochen Rindt. It is also a tribute to the skill and dedication of the mechanics who made the Lotus cars run, often under challenging conditions and with limited resources. Derek's book is a treasure trove of information and stories for anyone who loves racing history and wants to learn more about the inner workings of a successful and innovative team. I am honoured to have been part of Derek's journey and to share some of his experiences at Lotus, particularly those so instrumental in my early career as a professional race car driver. I hope you enjoy reading this book as much as I did.

Derek was a mechanic at Team Lotus from 1960 - 1964, and then my dedicated mechanic during my three-year Lotus contract which spanned 66 - 68 when he worked for Lotus Components/Developments.

Modern day professional racing teams now have an array of third, fourth or even more, contracted drivers in support of the two principal team drivers. Colin Champion, the owner of Lotus, chose me in my early career to sort of fill that role, unique then and a fantastic opportunity for me personally. Some race car constructors branched out into the burgeoning club racing market, producing lower formula race cars for the public — often selecting a smaller race team as a 'works team' to help promote their product. Colin formed Lotus Components as the division to produce a range of models, wherein I met Derek in my role as test driver and for the odd race.

From then on, in testing all manner of Lotus cars with Derek, I began to flourish in Formula 3 in 1966 as a dedicated one car team in full green and gold lotus livery — sometimes in a third car with Charles Lucas's works team with drivers Piers Courage and Boley Pittard. Derek, an employee of the company, became much more than just my mechanic; managing the programs on the cars back at base and at the circuits. He guided me as I progressed into the third driver role with Jim Clark and Graham Hill. With the help of Roger Frogley of Herts & Essex Aero Club, I drove a Formula 2 Lotus 48 with the new monocoque design for the European season and the Argentinian Temporada series in 1968. Some races I was in the third car with Jimmy and Graham. This was a combination of opportunity and support in my early career that Derek and I shared, and it paved the way for me to join Graham in the 1968 Formula 1 World Championship after Jimmy's fatal crash at Hockenheim in the Formula 2 Lotus.

© Peter Darley/JCT/CTL

Jackie Oliver, *Bedfordshire, May 2024*

Left to Right: *Ted Woodley,
Dennis London, Ian Seymoor,
Doug Bridge, Me, Cedric Selzer,
Jim Bull, Dick Scammell,
Trevor Taylor, Jim Endruweit,
Len Terry, Andrew Ferguson,
Sheila Gadd, ACBC, Bill Wells,
John Lambert, Keith Laine,
George Cooper, Roy Kemp,
George Holdaway, Mike Warne
and Jim Clark in the car.*

© London Express

"*This book is an insight into my 12 years working for Lotus,
and it tells of the blood, sweat and tears, as well as the
more humorous side that enabled us to 'let off steam'.*"

INTRODUCTION

This book is an insight into my 12 years working for Lotus, and it tells of the blood, sweat and tears, as well as the more humorous side that enabled us to 'let off steam'.

It begins with my introduction to motor racing at an early age and takes you through my time at the Cheshunt factory in Hertfordshire, then my move with the company to Hethel in Norfolk. I have put my take on the circuits that I worked at during my five years with the team, and later with Lotus Components and in Formula Two with the Herts and Essex Aero Club team. Many interesting, humorous, crazy and sometimes very sad things happened along the way.

My post-Lotus career with GRD, Modus and Van Diemen took me to many other circuits. I've included a few extremely memorable stories from this period but will go into more detail in a future book – God willing.

Jim Clark, Trevor Taylor, Jackie Oliver, Peter Arundell and John Miles are among the drivers I worked with. My fellow mechanics, friends and partners in crime have a chapter to themselves – deservedly so. I'm unable to name all of them, but the main Lotus F1 team of the early 1960s I worked alongside consisted of: Jim Endruweit (Chief Mechanic), Dick Scammell (who went on to be Director of Cosworth Engineering and received an MBE), David Lazenby, Colin Riley, Ted Woodley and Cedric Selzer.

Then there were the fitters, engineers, designers, photographers, race officials, journalists and everyone who made up the Grand Prix circus as it was then. Whilst in competition with drivers and teams from all over the world we managed to work in harmony most of the time, and I feel privileged to have worked under the technical genius of Colin Chapman, his designers and mechanics who

Early race circuit experience working on a Formula Junior.

"Now in my ninth decade, I felt it was time to reminisce about what was an important part of my life. I hope you have as much pleasure joining me down memory lane as I have had writing it."

continually pushed Team Lotus to the forefront of motor racing. It was an honour to have been a part of those early groundbreaking years.

Now in my ninth decade, I felt it was time to reminisce about what was an important part of my life. I hope you have as much pleasure joining me down memory lane as I have had writing it.

" *I imagine that oil started to seep into my bloodstream at an early age, when my father introduced me to the sport of motor racing by taking me along to Brands Hatch in Kent ... Little did I realise then that I would have the honour of working alongside some of these drivers, and many other great names in the sport in the years ahead.* "

An early appearance in Motoring News March 8th, 1962 as part of a two-page feature on Team Lotus by Mike Twite (M.L.T.). The better quality photo was sent to me by the Lotus designer, the late Ron Hickman.

My treasured Lotus Seven outside the family home in Mill Hill, 1960.

THE EARLY YEARS

I imagine that oil started to seep into my bloodstream at an early age, when my father introduced me to the sport of motor racing by taking me along to Brands Hatch in Kent to witness drivers like Jim Russell, Roy Salvadori, Stuart Lewis-Evans, Stirling Moss, David Boshier-Jones, Don Parker and Bob Gerard (always known in racing circles as 'Mr Bob'!) in action. They were competing in Formula Three cars powered by 500cc motorcycle engines, and were on the limits of adhesion around the famous, picturesque circuit. Little did I realise then that I would have the honour of working alongside some of these drivers, and many other great names in the sport in the years ahead.

The events of that day left me enthralled and greedy for more, so my father found himself taking me next to Goodwood on Easter Monday, 1956, where I was to witness my first fatality. A Tojeiro-Bristol sports car – given the name of the Sun-Pat Special (after the sponsors) – spun off the circuit at Lavant Corner and the driver, A.P.O. 'Bert' Rogers, was killed. It was at Goodwood that I first saw the flamboyant Mike Hawthorn complete a warm-up lap in a Connaught wearing a cheese cutter cap, with his blond hair flowing out from underneath!

In 1954, at the age of 16, I entered an engineering apprenticeship at the local Ford garage of W.H. Perry in North Finchley. Initially, I cycled to work, but it was boring and slow, so I acquired a 197cc Francis-Barnett motorcycle – not very cool – but all I could afford on my limited income. An added bonus was that it meant I could grab a few extra moments in bed before the 20-minute dash to

The petrol pumps at the front of W.H. Perry's. My first job as an apprentice mechanic.

Some of the new Ford stock for sale on the Forecourt.

Top: *A competition outing on my Francis-Barnett.* © Len Thorpe

Bottom: *I took my Dad's Ford Anglia 100E to a competition at Crystal Palace organised by the 750 Motor Club and won!*

work, where I would ride straight into the workshop to 'clock in'. This practice proved dangerous, as the floor was greasy and I often fell off, much to the amusement of my fellow workers (but not my boss!).

While riding home through Finchley one evening – exceeding the speed limit (as I often did in those days!) – I noticed a police motorcyclist out of the corner of my eye, kicking over his Triumph. I guessed he would be after me so, 'knowing it all', I decided to outrun him, turning left and right around the local roads. Suddenly, I felt a hand on my shoulder and was told to stop – Oh dear, my antics hadn't paid off and had only made matters worse! I had the biggest reprimand of my life and was made to feel very small, but managed to escape a ticket. Needless to say, I rode with a bit more care after that (for a while anyway!).

I progressed to a car after passing the driving test in my father's Ford Anglia 100E. I then used it as my transport to work, and also for my regular visits to the 750 Motor Club, which was a prominent group of enthusiasts that met at The Abbey Hotel, situated near the Brylcreem factory on the North Circular Road. Several members had modified cars or 'specials' and it wasn't long before the Anglia underwent a transformation, sporting twin front roll bars and lowered suspension, along with an Aquaplane cylinder head, twin carbs and a four-branch exhaust system! Journeys to and from these meetings often turned into a road race. I also used the Anglia to compete in some driving tests at Crystal Palace, and to my great surprise I actually won.

On one occasion, whilst returning from work during a very thick London fog, I was driving far too quickly for the conditions when I was pulled over (once again) by a police officer on his Triumph. He leaned in the car window and asked if I thought I was driving safely, to which my passenger and work colleague replied, "Safe as houses, been driving for years." This prompted the officer to remark, "World of experience eh, how long have you been driving?" I answered meekly, "One year, officer." I managed to get off (again) with a stern warning.

The car I really wanted and became desperate to own was the Lotus Seven, which I would ogle over at the 750 Club meetings. Eventually, I found one for sale in a car showroom. It was partly assembled, with only about a quarter of the work having been completed. After looking at it every night for three weeks, I managed to persuade my parents to help me purchase it. My friends all thought it was a load of aluminium scrap!

I towed my prize possession to a friend's garage and began to build a Ford 100E engine and gearbox from warranted parts courtesy of W.H. Perry that didn't make it back to the Ford factory in Dagenham!

The road holding and performance of the Seven was superb, but without a hood, side screens or heater it was extremely basic. When it rained you became very wet and, on acceleration, the water rushed up around your nether regions, only to rush back down to your feet on braking! 'Lotus Elbow' was a common feature as your right elbow was always hanging out of the side of the car. One trip to Yorkshire had me stopping at every café to thaw out, and finally arrive frozen and dirty. Needless to say, a hood and side screens were soon added!

A section of the Perry's workshop built large removal lorries, which were coach painted and clear varnished. Some of the vehicles went on to be signwritten, or had amazing artistic graphics such as scenery or specific products hand painted on them; it was a joy to see the craftsmanship involved in this work. Very soon my car was to undergo a transformation, when one of the enthusiastic painters offered to paint it a distinctive orange and grey with leftover paint from the lorries, so that it would stand out from the other Sevens. It certainly was an eye-catcher when finished.

As young apprentices we were always up to pranks (these were a good education for my years at Lotus!). In

the carpenters' shop was a large pit where all the offcuts of timber – along with sawdust and chippings – were kept to be taken away when the pit was full. Apprentices who completed their five-year term were thrown into the pit and covered with sawdust. This practice came to an abrupt halt when one young man, throwing handfuls of the sawdust at his fellow workmates, unfortunately missed and covered the side of a large truck that had just had its final coat of varnish.

I worked with George Cross, alias 'Diesel Dan', who rebuilt Thames Trader lorry engines. He was occasionally the subject of my pranks, when I would tap on a lorry with a small hammer as he started up the engine after a rebuild, leaving him less than amused. Once, after he had spent two or three days rebuilding an engine and refitting it into a lorry, I quietly placed a piston gudgeon pin circlip on his bench and watched him sweat until he realised what I'd done. This resulted in him chasing me around the entire workshop with a hammer.

We had a big concertina door into the main workshop to allow large lorries through, with a small personnel door in the middle. The boy from the butcher's came through every day to take meat to the canteen. Annoyingly, he always left the door open, even after being shouted at! So, he was taught a lesson by us fitting a large spring to the door. When he kicked it open it sprung back, knocking him and his tray of meat over. After that, we had no more problems with him.

The insurance assessor who came out to the garage always arrived on a bicycle. He would 'park' the said bicycle against the workbench and proceed to remove his cycle clips, then take out his clipboard from the saddle bag before getting down to business. He had a shock one day when he found his bicycle had disappeared from behind him – we had lifted it up to the factory roof by means of an electric – and very quiet – crane!

All apprentices attended Hendon College one day a

week, and students with exotic cars were asked to give the teachers a ride in them. My brother, Norman, had a friend who owned an Aston Martin DB4, which I used to fiddle about with, occasionally. I took it for a spin and managed to reach 120mph. On another occasion, I borrowed a friend's Lotus Eleven. This fine-looking car was very difficult to drive on the road as the streamlined body made the turning circle diabolical. Ground clearance was just four inches, so when approaching road works with an uneven surface it involved a 'ten-point turn' to turn around.

The handling was wonderful, as I found one day when passing the Ace Café (motorcycle H.Q. in those days). Three riders decided to chase me along the North Circular Road, riding right up behind me. I refused to lift off and flicked the Lotus through a roundabout, completely losing them. I often wondered if they fell off.

Also, while attending the college we occasionally worked on the instructors' cars (cheap labour for them). We did a few small jobs on a Ford Consul and then took it out on a 'test run', driving it flat as a tack, when suddenly there was a loud bang and the engine cut out. We sat terrified at what we had done, and contemplating the possible repercussions, when we realised that the large bunch of keys had swung on the ignition switch and cut out the engine – phew! We kept quiet of course.

Hendon taught us about the functions of the magneto (distributors and coils later replaced these), onto which we fitted a handle and could wind them up to produce quite a large spark. We would put several spanners along the workbench and then wind up the magneto so that the spark would jump from spanner to spanner, then ask another student to pass us a tool – which he duly did, giving him a large shock!

My first encounter with Colin Chapman was at Perrys, as they used to service his road cars. The vehicle we saw most frequently was the Raymond Mays converted Zephyr he used for towing his racing cars. There was also a Ford

Anglia, in which Mike Costin damaged his neck when it left the road as he was sleeping in the back seat. I can't remember who was behind the wheel.

With my apprenticeship coming to an end, I decided to look around for a more exciting career and spotted an advert to work on sports cars in the North London area. This turned out to be at the Lotus factory in Cheshunt, which I thought would be very handy as I could never manage to get spares for my Lotus Seven as the stores weren't open on Saturdays. I had an interview with Jim Endruweit, who was the Formula One Chief Mechanic, and it was at this point that I realised I would be working on the Formula One cars! Up until then, I assumed it would have been assembling the Lotus Elite or sports cars. You can imagine my excitement at the thought of being involved in the top line of the sport I loved and followed with enthusiasm. One of the tasks I had to complete to prove my ability was checking over the 2½-litre Coventry Climax engine used in the F1 cars – which I did successfully, and was thrilled to be told immediately that the job was mine, with Jim asking, "Can you start tomorrow?" I was on cloud nine as I drove away.

One of my first jobs was to spend a week in Coventry at Coventry Climax Engines learning the technique of topping and tailing the four-cylinder FPF engines, along with the smaller ones used in the Elite. Colin Chapman had noticed the attraction of the engines due to their light weight, with the early units having started life as fire pump engines. They were also used in the company's fork-lift trucks, before being modified for racing. The FPF was designed purely for racing purposes. Also, while I was there, I was introduced to Wally Hassan, Chief Engineer and Technical Director – who was also one of the Bentley Boys in his younger days – and Harry Spears, who was responsible for assembling and overhauling the customer engines. The pair came regularly to the circuits and worked closely with the teams.

The famous Coventry Climax engine I got to know rather well after starting at Lotus.

They had a test house where a full brake test was conducted. I was asked one day if I would like to actually go inside and watch, having viewed it previously through the window. The result was absolutely mind blowing and quite frightening. If you can imagine standing by a racing engine at full throttle, with the exhaust system glowing red hot and the water pipes – which were just held on with jubilee clips – flapping about. The noise was unbelievable, as there wasn't such a thing as ear defenders in those days.

In between full engine overhauls by Coventry Climax I would remove cylinder heads and sumps, plus check over the engine. I would work alone – apart from the company of scurrying rats – through the night on many occasions. After one exhausting night I tried to start the engine, but it wouldn't turn over and the car was due to go testing that afternoon. I removed the plugs and turned the engine over and four spurts of water shot out of the plug holes, hitting the ceiling – I had forgotten to put in the Cooper rings that should have been between the engine block and cylinder head. Panic ensued and I had to strip the engine

down very quickly and rebuild it – lesson learned!

The factory at Cheshunt had an engine test bed, which was managed by Steve Sanville, who worked with Bob Dance, Harry Gunn, Colin Gane and Nick Grimwood, testing all our own engines as well as development engines for other parts of the company, such as the Ford (Lotus) twin-cam, Vauxhall (Lotus) twin-cam, V8 Ford for the type 30/40 sports racing cars and also a V8 for the proposed Indianapolis project. The latter was bolted onto the test bed before being installed in the Lotus 29 monocoque, ready for testing at Snetterton by Jim Clark. Engineers controlled the programme from outside the test house, viewing through a glass window. The engine ran for many hours with the original exhaust system of eight short pipes which finished just above the carburettor line. This was a temporary measure until the latest crossover system (similar to F1) arrived from V.W. Derrington of London. The crossover pipes from the exhaust fitted well, but the two tailpipes proved to be a problem as they were too long for our small test house. Colin was consulted and he

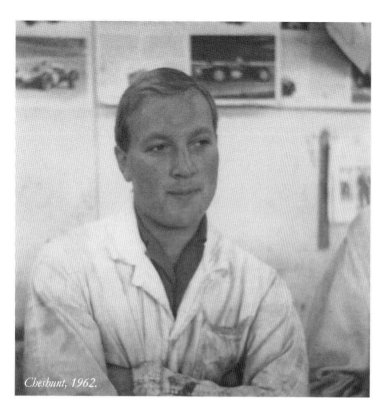
Cheshunt, 1962.

magnesium. Machining them created quite a problem. When the lathe tip became blunt it would ignite the shavings, which would burn furiously with a bright white light. The only way to extinguish the fire would be to starve it of oxygen by covering it with sand.

Charlie, the local rag and bone man, kept his horse in a field next to the factory, which was upsetting to see as most of the time the poor thing stood in water with very little to eat. Despite attempts to point this out to him our pleas were ignored, so we took matters into our own hands and untethered it, leaving it to wander into the factory estate road. We then rang the police, and the RSPCA came out and caught it, reprimanding Charlie, which resulted in him getting better accommodation for his horse.

The Lotus fabrication shop built panels for the Sevens and most of the racing and sports cars. They also constructed Colin's innovative design for the first monocoque to be used in Formula 1 cars. It was interesting to watch the four very skilled and experienced craftsmen working on these projects. The problem was, they were a very tight-knit group belonging to a union, unlike the rest of us. So, while we worked in cold conditions and were hungry with no breaks, they would have regular tea breaks and hot sausages cooked on their stove in the workshop. We would smell these, and our mouths would water! Colin would walk past us and mutter, "Bloody communists." He didn't approve of unions, and after many years of dispute he decided to sack them all. Initially, the work then went to an outside firm that had all the patterns passed on to them. When cutting out the panels for the Sevens they realised they had mysteriously shrunk! Don't mess with union members!

In 1962, while working on the 1.5-litre V8 Coventry Climax engines, which went back to them for rebuild, I was sent over to Lake Constance in Germany to learn how to maintain the five-speed DS10 Zahnradfabrik Friedrichshafen (ZF) gearboxes we were using. The factory

instructed the maintenance department to remove a few bricks from the wall to allow the pipes to protrude outside into the nearby field.

More tests followed, and so did the complaints from nearby offices, including those from Tesco headquarters, which was situated opposite us on Delamere Road. Eventually, Colin told the maintenance department to build a chimney over the protruding exhaust tailpipes to try and dampen the noise. This worked for a while, until the engineers were completing some engine tests, which unfortunately allowed petrol vapour to accumulate. The next time they started up the engine there was a huge explosion that blew down the chimney. At this point they decided to carry on regardless, much to the annoyance of our neighbours!

Directly opposite the factory was Heldrew Engineering who machined our wheels, which were usually made from

The ZF gearbox. Another component I came to know well.

was enormous; they made gearboxes and differentials for all industries, including shipping and automotive. I was there for a few days working with their engineers, who were a mixture of nationalities due to the factory being on the border with Switzerland and Italy. Most of them did about six hours at ZF and then worked elsewhere in the evening. The gearbox we used was originally designed for an off-road, four-wheel drive vehicle. They were well made and were of a synchromesh design – it wasn't possible to change intermediate gear ratios – which meant you could only change the final drive crown wheel and pinion (a lot of work for me!). We would carry about six gearboxes in the transporter, with a choice of three different final drives, to the races. Once I had acquired the necessary information I returned to Cheshunt to work on the gearboxes and was assigned to the spare car at the races.

The Zeppelin airships were built by the lake and in the middle was a mooring post to attach them to. There was also a Zeppelin museum by the lake. Years later, I revisited Lake Constance and popped into the factory, but wasn't able to get far because of security!

I'm sat in a type 23 outside the factory at Cheshunt. The sports-racers were often tested on the A10 in Hertfordshire, using trade plates, much to the approval of local enthusiasts. Needless to say, the police took a different view.

2

THE HUMOROUS SIDE OF RACING

A usual day for race mechanics started at 8.30am and finished on average around 9.30pm. Also usual were many 'all-nighters', sometimes on consecutive nights, followed by driving the transporter to the circuits. All these hours of hard work often resulted in stupid pranks to relieve the tedium. Looking back, it would have been more productive to have had four hours sleep and then returned to work rather than to continue and be only 30% efficient.

The management decided to supply us with music day and night, with varying tunes to keep us alert, but after hearing the tape over and over, especially late at night, it was agreed to shoot it down. Pop rivets in a brake bundy tube with compressed air entering at one end of it soon silenced the awful droning noise.

In the production shop close to the fabrication area a coffee/tea machine was installed but many of the staff thought that the price was far too high, so it was left to those of us with imagination to source a way of obtaining free drinks. Long pieces of welding wire along with a scratching of heads soon produced a method of supplying us our drinks at no cost. The vending company – realising something was wrong – came along and monitored it, saying it was impossible to beat (not at Lotus though!). Eventually, after several modifications, they admitted defeat and the machine was removed.

Oxy-acetylene bombs were a great source of amusement to us all. We could make these in anything from plastic cups to dustbin liners, and they would explode with a large bang and yellow flash.

Oxy-acetylene bombs were a great source of amusement to us all. We could make these in anything from plastic cups to dustbin liners, and they would explode with a large bang and yellow flash. One night we were still working well past midnight when someone mentioned to David 'Laz' Lazenby (first-class bomb maker), that we ought to make a big one. A bag the size of a dustbin liner was filled with oxy-acetylene and a petrol-soaked string was made ready. There was snow on the ground and thick fog as the 'bomb' was placed on the grass outside the Heldrew Engineering factory opposite Lotus and the fuse duly lit. We retired to the race shop to await the outcome but after several minutes nothing had happened. Laz was forced out into the passage between the team and production factories to investigate. He crept out to stand behind a lamp post and indicated that the fuse was still burning. By this time we were all standing in the passage when

That's ace bombmaker David Lazenby's Lotus 17 by the Test House at Cheshunt. A customer's single-seater is awaiting attention.

suddenly there was an almighty bang which cleared the fog and blew away about 20 feet of snow. Unfortunately, it also blew out some of our factory windows. Lights in Cheshunt went on and the police arrived! Of course, we were all hard at work and hadn't heard anything. A.C.B.C. (Anthony Colin Bruce Chapman – 'The Gov' or 'Chunky' as he was sometimes known) was not a happy man the next day.

Speaking of Colin brings to mind an incident when he owned a 3.8-litre Jaguar and, as an ex-racing driver, you can imagine how he pushed that! I was sitting at the traffic lights in my Lotus Seven waiting with others to turn right towards Enfield town centre when I saw this green Jag roaring up behind me. He pulled over to the right side of the road, passing us all and waving (with two fingers) as he did so, gaining about 30 seconds on us.

Life wasn't always easy working for Colin, and it was sometimes difficult to know what was the best thing to do, as I knew well – such as the day I told him the cars were prepared, ready for his inspection, before we loaded them onto the transporter. Looking underneath he asked, "Who didn't paint the fabricated engine mounts?" I owned up

and he shouted loudly at me (to put it politely) giving me a right ear bashing before dashing off to speak to Mike Costin. I quickly masked up the surrounding area and sprayed them, hoping to get into his good books but no... On his return, he again shouted at me saying, "Never paint things in situ." Ho-hum!

In the workshop was a three-tier tubular racing tyre rack which was filled with oxy-acetylene by John Lambert, one of the development staff, and then lit with a welding torch. As I was working by this rack I took the full impact and was deaf for the next two days. The fabrication and development shop was on the upper floor and they were experimenting with hydrogen, so what next, but to fill one balloon with oxy-acetylene and the other with hydrogen then tie them together with string and a Jetex fuse. This was released into the night sky over Cheshunt with the usual results and another visit from the Constabulary!

> *In the workshop was a three-tier tubular racing tyre rack which was filled with oxy-acetylene by John Lambert, one of the development staff, and then lit with a welding torch. As I was working by this rack I took the full impact and was deaf for the next two days.*

Nobody escaped the dreaded 'bomb', not even Jeff our security guard who had one go off in his bicycle saddle bag. Jeff was inclined to the odd joke himself and would often pretend to search us as we went past his security hut to and from work. He had second thoughts about his pranks after one day when he pretended to spar box with a tough, stocky lorry driver who was delivering to us. The chap failed to see the funny side and laid Jeff out before driving off.

An innocent welding torch in the wrong hands could

provide some amusement when put into a dustbin in full view of the drawing office above our workshop. After a few minutes, a face would appear anxiously at the window followed by another, then another two, then the noise of pattering feet as all the drawing office staff ran out of the building. Mike Costin, who was in charge of the office and greatly respected, came rushing into the team workshop demanding an explanation. When told that the torch 'had just been laid down' he took the joke well.

When on the very rare occasions work was a little slow mischief would abound and a hot mix of fibreglass and resin thrown into the works rubbish dump soon livened things up and brought out the Cheshunt fire brigade.

A wedding was always another opportunity to test our skills, so when a colleague was about to get married I decided to tie an old pair of trousers to the back of his car as a joke. He didn't find them for several days but when he did he paid me back by wiring my Cortina GT's hooters to a switch underneath the car and attaching a piece of string loosely around the prop shaft. Completely oblivious to this deed, I jumped in and drove off only to find that after driving a few yards the hooters started sounding continuously, so with much embarrassment I opened the bonnet and pulled the wires off the hooters. It was only later that I realised what had happened – nice one!

Sometimes a prank would go wrong, such as on the occasion when Colin Gane and Bob Dance, who worked in the engine development shop, returned from a trip to the Nürburgring 1000kms sports car race where they had overseen the new Lotus twin-cam engine fitted to the works Lotus 23 sports racing car. The car driven by Jim Clark and Trevor Taylor had outpaced all of the larger-engined sports cars from Porsche and Ferrari and by the eighth lap, Jim had a lead of over two minutes. Unfortunately, the exhaust manifold cracked allowing fumes into the cockpit affecting his judgement and he fell off!

Top: *While we were always up for a laugh, we did work hard. A completed type 25 outside the factory, while behind work continues on the new building that would be the home of Lotus Cortina production.*

Bottom: *Butter wouldn't melt?*

Upon Colin's return from the 'Ring', he noticed that the stick-on windscreen demister from his Rover had been stolen. After checking all the cars in the car park and on the road where some had to park, he found it on an old Ford Prefect (the type with the alligator bonnet and headlights on top of the front wings). Having decided to teach the owner a lesson a small bomb was fitted on top of the engine with the spark plug lead used to ignite it. Just before 5pm, the device was checked but it had deflated so a bigger one was prepared and installed with several of us sitting in an old van close to the action. An elderly man came out of the factory and approached the car. As he switched on the ignition there was an almighty bang resulting in the bonnet being blown open, the sides bent around the headlight, and a damaged battery. The poor driver was shaken and soon the police, ambulance and fire brigade arrived. The police interviewed most of the factory, but fortunately not the team. It was then decided that these activities must stop.

Team Lotus were not the only mechanics to get up to pranks. An event springs to mind of when one of the Cooper mechanics, Noddy (Michael) Grohmann, told us how he once filled an inner tube with oxy-acetylene but had not had time to set it off so placed it in the back of his Minivan with the intention of removing it later – but completely forgot. November 5th came and he organised a bonfire with fireworks for his children. When this was over and the sausages duly eaten the children went off to bed while Noddy settled himself down in front of the glowing embers. He suddenly remembered the tube, so casually removed it from the van and flung it on the embers, before returning to his kitchen. There was an almighty bang that blew out several windows in his house.

The racing sports cars were tested on the A10 in Hertfordshire, using trade plates. This created a magnificent sight for enthusiasts but not the local police. Sometimes for lunch, we would all go to a transport café on the A10 known as The Orange Café. This always resulted in a race, usually won by David Lazenby in his Lotus Seventeen. He built the car himself using a Renault gearbox found in a French scrap yard on our way back from the Grand Prix. The rear uprights were fabricated using much-machined Lucas dynamo housings as bearing carriers. He was a brilliant engineer and after leaving Lotus founded Hawke Racing Cars, and achieved some great results in FF1600 and FF2000. Sadly, Laz passed away at 86 years of age in January 2023. Other 'competitors' included Cedric Selzer in a Lotus Seven, Dick Scammell in an old Crossley, Harry Gunn from the engine shop in an E-type Jaguar, and one of the fitters from Lotus Components (I forget his name, which is probably for the best!), who was very quick in a much-modified Ford Anglia 105E, which was thanks to Lotus, but not I believe to their knowledge.

> **The racing sports cars were tested on the A10 in Hertfordshire, using trade plates. This created a magnificent sight for enthusiasts but not the local police.**

Sometimes we would also eat at a small café in Waltham Abbey, a small town close to Cheshunt. The drawback with this place was the owner's small Pekingese dog, which we nicknamed 'Snuffy' because it was always snuffling around our feet for scraps. A sandwich containing salt, pepper, sauce, etc... was made and put down to be devoured by the greedy hound. The next day we asked about its whereabouts and were told it had not been very well (sorry to all dog lovers!).

The racing Cortina shop was situated next to the race team in the factory. This proved extremely useful when a pogo stick became the next invention. A Lotus Cortina

The Elite of Ron Buxton parked outside the Cheshunt factory below Colin's office where a Kiwi, who worked in the production shop, and lived only 100 yards from the factory, would bid goodnight to A.C.B.C, while walking home on a pair of six-foot stilts.

front coil spring was the ideal part and a later Mk2 version had two springs welded together on it and could be made to jump to five feet by the very brave. Ray Parsons, our Australian engineer, who also drove an Elan for us, proved to be the best until he sprained his wrists when landing on the ground.

The pogo adventure then spurned thoughts on to making a pair of stilts. A pair of four-foot ones proved a bit too mundane so six-foot ones were constructed. One of our production shop Kiwis tried them out and became

quite proficient. As he lived only 100 yards from the factory he chose to walk home on them, passing A.C.B.C.'s first-floor office and bidding him goodnight through the window. Dismounting was extremely dangerous and sprained ankles eventually forced a stop to the stilt programme.

Team Lotus moved to Hethel, Norfolk, in 1966 and we were soon getting itchy fingers, so not a bomb, but a cannon was designed. A thick-walled aluminium tube was found and a small bracket was attached near to the

My Austin-Healey alongside a type 23 at Cheshunt.

bottom. We dug out a sugar beet and having trimmed it to size fitted it in the tube which was then ignited. The sugar beet shot up in the air to about 100 feet, but just at that moment the local postman happened to be cycling by and was narrowly missed. For the next cannon, we turned up a 3-inch diameter shell on the lathe. This was fired across a field and took a branch out of a tree before landing near some cows. It probably affected their milk yield for days.

Do you remember Jeff the security guard from Cheshunt? He moved up with us and security became much tighter with proper fencing and a gatehouse instead of a hut. At night he would do his rounds of the factory, clocking in at various points. We often worked late and sometimes all night so decided to liven things up by sending a young lad out to hide behind some crates that he would pass. Just as we thought, Jeff spotted him but, not

realising who he was, crept around following him until we all jumped out to give him a bit of a fright. He still liked to show his authority at the gate and one day made the big mistake of trying to stop Colin Chapman – this was taking his role to the limit and proved to be the case when an angry boss crashed through the barrier in disgust.

Lunchtime Olympics was the next series of events, involving such feats as seeing how many driveshafts someone could lift and hold for two minutes. Tired and sprained muscles meant these activities were short-lived.

While on the subject of lunchtime, the canteen lunches were always particularly good. It was well known that I had (and still have) a liking for tomato sauce and in those days would use it liberally on everything. One particular day, I found that the sauce in the bottle was exceptionally stubborn in coming out. Even a knife wouldn't budge it, so I took it back to complain, only to realise that I had been 'set up' by fibreglass expert Alan Barrett, who had filled the bottle with a tomato coloured fibreglass mix.

Birthdays were a time of celebration for us, so when we found out it was the turn of young Irish mechanic Eamon Fullalove we bound him hand and foot with tank tape before hanging him up on the engine lifting crane and then taking him into the open plan offices and depositing him onto the desks of the Team Lotus secretaries. He was a lot quieter after this embarrassing event.

I'm sat in Jimmy's car at the secret Milwaukee test.

"Once the cars were ready for testing we moved on to the Milwaukee oval. We were fortunate to be able to work at the premises of the Zecol Lubaid stock car team, whose main driver was Jimmy Hurtubise."

③

CIRCUIT TALES – PART ONE
USA, MEXICO, SOUTH AFRICA AND ARGENTINA

MILWAUKEE

In 1963, I was asked to go to America and work at Ford's Dearborn Experimental and Development factory on the two Lotus 29 Indy cars designed by Len Terry. These were the cars with offset suspension and a Ford V8 4.2 litre engine. I flew out along with Colin Riley – a fellow mechanic – and we were booked into a motel and given a Ford Thunderbird to drive about in. My idea of heaven!

We prepared the cars in a workshop near the engine and transmission test rooms where the Ford Motor Company had been running the V8s continuously for many weeks. Trying to get some tools from the Ford stores department was as bad as asking for a new hacksaw blade from Lotus!

While there we managed to get some time off (Colin Chapman wasn't there chasing!) so we went to see some powerboat racing on Lake Michigan. These boats were capable of speeds up to 200mph and lifted about 40 feet of spray behind them; the acceleration was incredible.

We also managed a quick visit to Henry Ford's Museum in Dearborn. This was the biggest museum I had ever seen. Henry collected everything from cars and boats to aeroplanes and railway engines – even a homemade armoured car that had crashed through a checkpoint in the Eastern Bloc. In the grounds was his wooden house that he was born in and a lake, complete with Mississippi

The Ford Thunderbird loaned to us by the Dearborn factory during our visit in 1963.

paddle steamer giving rides, while on the roads Model T Fords were driving around. He had also bought the workshops of the engineers who had started with him in the early days, such as electricians and bicycle wheel manufacturers. A truly fantastic place to visit. Before we left Dearborn we were given a very exciting ride around the test track by the Ford engineers in a 7-litre convertible, which included driving up a 45-degree slope.

Once the cars were ready for testing we moved on to the Milwaukee oval. We were fortunate to be able to work at the premises of the Zecol Lubaid stock car team, whose

The Ford of Jim Hurtubise.

main driver was Jimmy Hurtubise. It was interesting to see the engineers heating up the car frame to be able to add camber to the front suspension.

The circuit was hired by Ford so that the two cars of Jim Clark and Dan Gurney could be tested and their set-ups sorted for the race later in the year. It was a very hot day and was supposed to be a secret test session, but news must have leaked out and there were around 2,000 spectators in the stand opposite the pit area – some of them with bagpipes and kilts! Jim took the time to go across and speak to them.

It's worth mentioning that his car was in traditional Lotus team colours, which upset the superstitious Americans as green was considered an unlucky colour. Dan's was acceptable as his was in the American racing colours of white with a blue stripe. Both cars did several laps and Jim was quickest, with Dan very close behind.

Because of this he wanted to change some of the settings, but Chapman insisted that the car be left as it was as Dan's ideas probably wouldn't have worked.

Our Indy cars had four-speed gearboxes as opposed to the American Roadster Indy cars with only two-speed boxes, which gave us a tremendous advantage. Colin Riley and I worked on the cars for a while and then had to sit in the air-conditioned large estate car to cool down as it was so hot.

While the cars were in the pit area, Hurtubise did a few laps in his Ford Galaxie stock car before offering Jimmy a drive. He thoroughly enjoyed the experience and put in some impressive times, much to the delight of the spectators.

It was interesting to hear Dan explaining to me the various aerodynamic effects of the different stock cars racing at circuits like Daytona, where cars reach 200mph,

Dan Gurney climbs aboard, while in the distance, Jimmy takes the Nascar Ford of Jim Hurtubise for a spin.

NO "SMOKING IN" PIT AREA

Dan's type 29.

Above: *Colin Riley and I pose with Jimmy's car.*

Top right: *Henry Ford's house.*

Bottom right: *One of the many model Ts being driven around the museum grounds.*

and how it was vital to know the turbulent effects of each model to enable the driver behind to pass safely and not be sucked into the trunk (boot) or the side.

I had to fly to the Indianapolis Motor Speedway for some spares and whilst there was offered food and drink from an American mechanic whose work consisted of preparing an Offenhauser-engined Indy car. He practically lived in the garage with his own fridge, stove and even a television! The car was an old fashioned, front-engined 'Roadster' with a huge steel-tubed chassis. The driver sat bolt upright in front of a massive fuel tank – similar to a Maserati 250F. This type of design was soon rendered obsolete when we (Lotus) showed them the modern

way to build quick cars. It was surprising they hadn't taken notice previously in 1961, when Jack Brabham had competed in the '500' driving a rear-engined 2.7-litre Cooper-Climax. His impressive performance gave an early indication that the British/European way of building/ designing racing cars was on its way across the pond.

Noddy Grohmann, the Cooper mechanic who worked on Jack's car, arrived at the Speedway and promptly emptied the contents of his small toolbox onto the floor of the garage and started work – much to the amazement of the American mechanics, who had immaculate, upright and very expensive toolboxes. Just goes to show that equipment isn't everything.

An Offenhauser-engined Roadster minus its body at the Indianapolis Speedway. It sure looks outdated compared to the Lotus.

WATKINS GLEN

A picturesque venue north of New York near the Finger Lakes. The Grand Prix was late in the season, so arriving in the 'fall' (autumn) the trees were turning gold, making a beautiful backdrop.

Our visit in 1964 drew a large crowd (around 60,000), that included many Canadians from across the border. The organisation was always good, with friendly officials and police. A new scrutineering building was in use and the Race Controller, Cameron Argetsinger, allowed us to prepare the cars in it. The night watchman was a charming elderly policeman who carried a loaded pistol, which he informed us he would have no hesitation in using if necessary. We hoped that he didn't become too excited in his mission, and as a precaution our usual antics were thwarted! But he did make a lovely cup of tea.

We stayed in a chalet in the grounds of the Seneca Lodge Hotel complex by the lake. The town of Watkins Glen looked as if it was straight out of an American western film, with wooden shops down either side of the main street, their verandahs projecting out onto the sidewalks. One could almost imagine a cowboy riding his horse down the street. By 9.30pm the town was dead, so most evenings we amused ourselves by sitting beside the lake making model cars, but one night we did drive many miles to watch a demolition derby event.

All the teams had Ford Mustangs supplied by Ford USA for our own use during our stay. There were probably about 30 in total, all identical in white with two blue strips running from the front to the rear.

Dan Gurney showed us how to get wheelspin for as long as we wished – well at least until the tyres started to melt! It was a combination of holding the V8 on full

One of the 30 Ford Mustangs loaned to the F1 teams to use during the Watkins Glen meeting.

For the 1964 Grand Prix we entered a third car for Walt Hansgen, a talented American sportscar racer. Here in a somewhat cramped debrief, Walt chats with Jimmy, Mike (Spence), Colin, and Dick (Scammell). It looks as though the two guys with their back to the camera are filming the whole thing.

power and releasing the brakes slowly to allow one wheel to spin until smoking; then fully release the brake to get both rears smoking. This could be driven for half a mile, causing great amusement. The wide road leading to the circuit was ideal for us to drag race against the Mustangs of BRM and Coopers.

The speed limit around the town was 25mph, so the local police were kept quite busy trying to enforce law and order amongst us in these identical cars. Graham Hill and Dan Gurney had a bet as to who could reverse up the steep grassy bank by the hotel. Dan won the bet.

On a rare day off, we were able to visit Niagara Falls and set off along with the BRM mechanics in the aforementioned Mustangs. Dick Scammell, who had been to the Falls before, warned us not to exceed the speed limit of 50mph as the police were quite strict. Initially, observing the speed limit was okay, but after many miles at that laborious speed – especially on large motorway type roads in a car capable of 130mph – I became a little bored so I gave it the gun. A few miles later I passed a car whose driver was in uniform with a badge on the sleeve, which didn't bother me too much; I thought he was a petrol pump attendant! Until further along the road I was pulled over by

the police and we were all told the get out of the car and stand by the side with our hands on the roof. I was severely reprimanded to put it mildly, but after explaining in my best English accent that we were working at the Grand Prix and due to fly back to England the next day he let me off, which was just as well as he was bristling with guns!

> **"The speed limit around the town was 25mph, so the local police were kept quite busy trying to enforce law and order amongst us in these identical cars."**

Niagara was brilliant and we put on waterproofs to go through a tunnel emerging at the base of the waterfall. We all came out soaking wet as there was tremendous spray.

The race was won by Graham Hill in the BRM from John Surtees in his Ferrari. It meant that either one of them would be crowned champion at the final round in Mexico. Jimmy had been on pole but retired on lap 45 due to fuel injection problems. The chequered flag was waved by the white-suited Tex Hopkins in his normal flamboyant manner.

With the next race being in Mexico, we stayed in Watkins Glen for a week preparing the cars and helping to load them onto trucks to be transported south. During the week we drove to Pennsylvania to watch a very entertaining drag meeting at Pocono Drag Lodge. Some of the dragster engines were filled with concrete to stop them bursting. A free fall parachute display team all landed on the strip within ten feet of each other, which was very impressive. All the team then drove to New York, where we visited the Empire State Building. The lifts ascended at a tremendous speed and the views from the top were breathtaking.

We found out that flying from New York to Mexico gave us the opportunity to visit Acapulco for three days courtesy of the airline – great! We had a super hotel overlooking the bay and were soon down on the beach, where the water temperature was like a bath. It was a well needed break and thoroughly enjoyed – well almost, as unfortunately, when I went waterskiing, I stepped off my skis straight on top of a large sea urchin. I was left with thousands of broken off spines in my foot. If that wasn't bad enough the locals said it was necessary to hit my foot with a piece of wood so that the poison would come out. After a couple of Tequilas this was done and I began hobbling about in much pain.

We flew back to Mexico City in a small plane with two propeller driven engines. As we were flying over a mountain range the pilot kept reducing speed and turning lights onto the wings and engines. Snow was falling heavily and I believe that the wings must have been icing up. When he reduced speed further we were beginning to get rather concerned, but eventually managed to reach our destination safely.

We found out later that Jimmy also had problems in the small plane taking him to Mexico. The landing gear had failed and had to be operated manually.

MEXICO

Mexico City stands 7,400 feet above sea level and the circuit (the Autodromo) was a short drive from our hotel in the centre. The drive was through some of the poorest areas, with people sleeping in cardboard boxes and makeshift homes. This was a sharp contrast to the glamour and wealth of the circuit.

We arrived after our hairy flight and drove in our hire car to unload the racing cars from the transporters that had driven down from Watkins Glen. This was very difficult for me as my foot was extremely painful and swollen due to the sea urchin episode, and still had many spines in it despite the wood bashing! One of the Cooper mechanics had dropped a jack on his foot, so we hobbled about together.

We once again found ourselves in trouble with the police when we jumped a traffic light at a main road junction. The policeman reprimanded us and demanded cash, which we didn't give him, so he then demanded our passports. Dick Scammell said no way were we going to do that. Fortunately for us, a senior officer arrived and the proceedings were explained to him and he allowed us to drive off. Not long after that incident we were caught out again by the traffic lights, but this time braked heavily and skidded to a halt. The senior officer from the earlier incident – who happened to be there – looked around and gave us the thumbs up.

The pit area was about 20 paces from the track itself, so I sat on one of the straw bales with the lap/time board and signalled to our cars after the times were shouted to me from the pit counter where Colin Chapman was busy with his stopwatches.

The altitude was causing many problems for the mechanics, as well as affecting the performance of the cars due to the thinner air. Everything became an effort. Just running down to the pits or pushing a car left one breathless and exhausted. The fuel mixtures had to be reduced and the cars lost 25-30bhp. Also, tyre pressures had to be reduced to 4/5 lb per square inch. With track temperatures at 110 degrees Fahrenheit it was also affecting the drivers, who couldn't afford to make too many mistakes and hit the straw bales that defined the track boundary, as in Zeltweg.

Before the race the drivers were presented to Adolf López Mateos, the President of Mexico, after which thousands of balloons and hundreds of doves were sent off into the sky followed by a small aeroplane flying in and bursting the balloons. Fortunately, the doves had by then flown well away – quite spectacular!

"The altitude was causing many problems for the mechanics, as well as affecting the performance of the cars due to the thinner air. Everything became an effort."

For this race I was working on the car of Mike Spence. After the warming up lap he came on to the grid waving his arms (not a good sign!). Chapman said that he had damaged the nose and couldn't select the gears properly. I quickly taped up the nose with tank-tape and inspected the gear-shift mechanism, but nothing seemed to be wrong. By then, Chapman was pacing up and down saying "Fix it, fix it!" Luckily, during the race the gear selection worked perfectly – the problem was put down to over-enthusiasm – and Mike finished in fourth place.

In an eventful race over 65 laps (201 miles) to decide the championship, Hill was hit up the rear by the Ferrari – resplendent in the white and blue livery of the North America Racing Team (NART) – of Lorenzo Bandini, which bent the exhaust of the BRM. After the race Bandini did go to the BRM pits and apologise. Towards the end Gurney was leading Bandini with Surtees in

third place, which wasn't good enough for him to win the championship. If he could pass his team-mate and finish second he would become the first man to be world champion on both two and four wheels. On the penultimate lap, when Bandini came past the pit area, the Ferrari Team Manager waved to him to slow down and let Surtees past. He responded with two fingers (possibly meaning he was in second place!). When he came past to start the final lap drastic action was called for, and his team virtually stood in front of him to allow Surtees past to claim the championship. Gurney was a worthy race winner and the crowd were wondering why everyone was congratulating Surtees and not him.

The next morning we all met up in the hotel reception to pay our bills, before driving to the airport for the journey home. Chapman arrived from the lift as we prepared to leave, only to find that he had left his passport in his room on the fifth floor. He rushed back to the lift to go and retrieve it. We knew he suffered from claustrophobia and we could stop the lift between floors with a piece of paper strategically wedged through the edge of the doors. This was done as the lift was descending and we could hear him banging and shouting from within. After a couple of minutes the paper was removed and the lift continued down, with a very red and flustered passenger stumbling out – much to the amusement of us all!

At the airport, Colin, in his usual way, dashed between the various airline desks and said we could transfer our flights to get home sooner. We all decided to stay with our original arrangements, so Colin dashed off to catch an 'earlier' flight. We arrived back in the UK four hours ahead of him!

We used to count up the seconds from start to lift off when flying around the world, usually in Boeing 707s, but when leaving Mexico the take-off was unusually long and this gave us cause for some concern, until we realised that we took off in thin air as we were already at 7,400 feet!

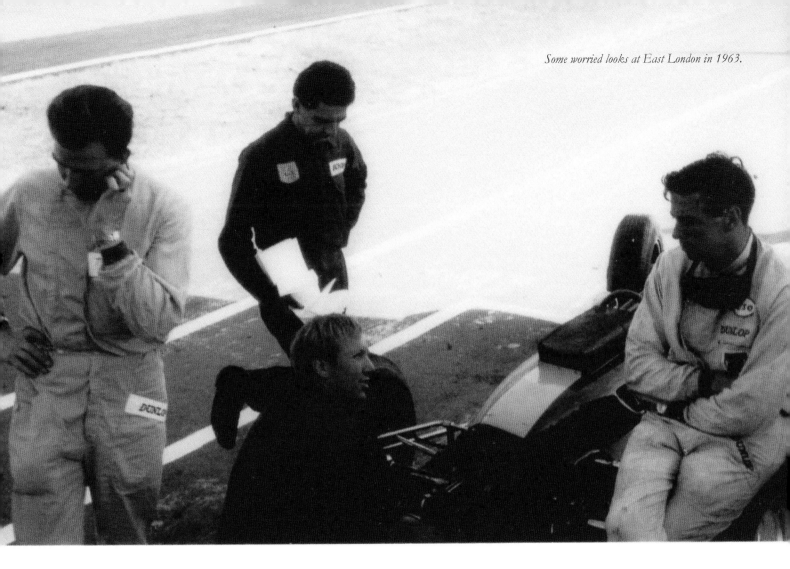

KYALAMI AND EAST LONDON

Christmas 1963 in South Africa sounded too good to miss, with one race at Kyalami near Johannesburg and another at the East London circuit, which was on the coast overlooking the Indian Ocean.

The cars and all the equipment had to be transported to Southampton to be loaded onto a ship bound for South Africa. With the two cars loaded up onto the Bedford transporter – and with an open backed lorry carrying spares – Cedric and I set off at 3am on a very cold November morning after having lit a fire underneath the diesel tank to warm up the fuel as it had frozen, which makes it jellified. As well as the cold we had to endure thick fog on the way down that was lying about five feet above the road, which meant the car drivers couldn't see – but as we were sitting higher it wasn't a problem for us. This led to a very frustrating and laborious journey. Upon arrival we discovered the dock workers were on a 'go slow' and refused to get a forklift to enable us to unload the cars and spares. Even an offer of photos and badges couldn't entice them, so we had a huge struggle to unload all of our equipment.

Doug Bridge, myself, Cedric, and
Colin seem happier in this photo.

It was cold and snowing when we flew out from
Heathrow aboard the usual Boeing 707, accompanied by
most of the other teams and drivers. During the flight we
were allowed to visit the cockpit and sit in the navigator's
seat, while two of the drivers (I can't remember who)
actually had the privilege to sit in the co-pilot's seat. The
captain brought the plane down low enough over Africa
for us to see the wild animals below.

We landed at Entebbe airport in Uganda to refuel. Even
though it was night time we were hit by the tremendous
heat when the doors opened, so we had to strip off all our
layers of winter clothes that we had left England in. The
airport lounge area was just a shack and we had a long
wait for the aircraft to be refuelled. It was done using an

immaculate new fuel tanker which put fuel into the aircraft
and then drove off behind some sheds, where we saw it
being filled up with several men carrying jerry cans! We
arrived in Johannesburg and found that the cars had been
transported on a very large low loader, making them look
quite small in comparison. We were to work on the cars in
a local garage and drive them to the circuit.

Colin Chapman was not attending as it was not a
world championship Grand Prix, so it was a more relaxed
atmosphere. We had four days to prepare the cars, so
when the South African driver Tony Maggs and his wife
Gail invited us to water ski on the lake behind their superb
thatched bungalow situated in a hilly area a few miles from
the circuit, we jumped at the chance. Cedric (who is also

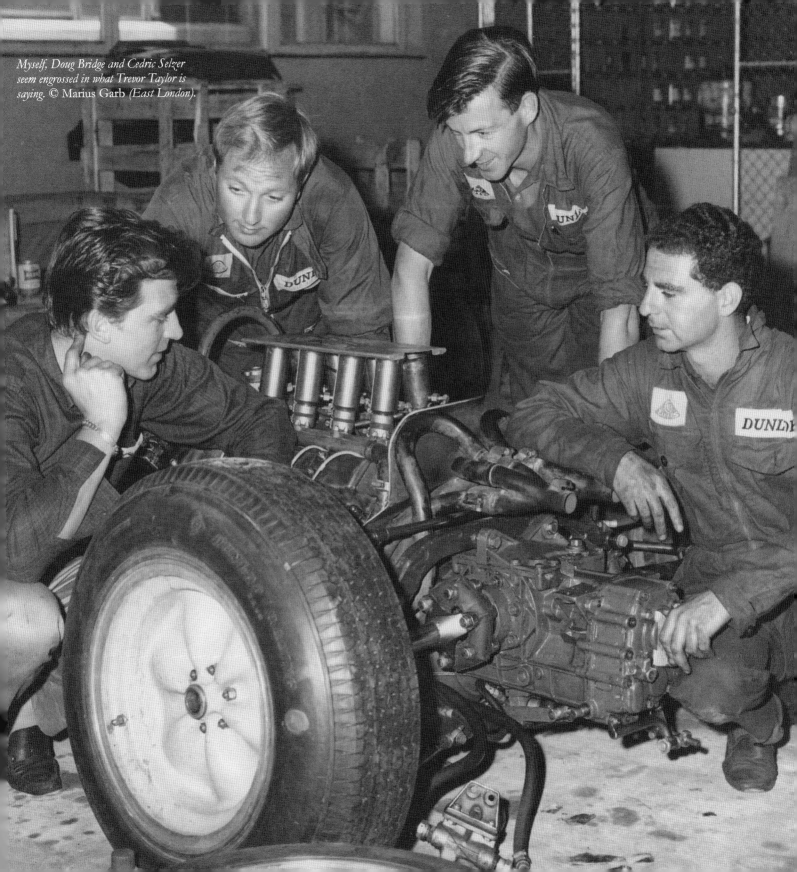

Myself, Doug Bridge and Cedric Selzer seem engrossed in what Trevor Taylor is saying. © Marius Garb (East London).

South African), myself, Jimmy and Trevor all used to start work on the cars at 6am, so that by early afternoon we could down tools and rush up to the lake along with Mike Hailwood, Bruce McLaren and his wife, Pat.

The lake was fairly green due to a floating weed, and if you accidentally drank some it was possible to get a disease called bilharzia, which was carried by snails. We had a great time and partied well into the night with many other drivers, including the local racers, John Love and Peter de Klerk. One evening, John's pal arrived straight from work in his suit and promptly rolled up his trouser legs and skied straight off the jetty to complete four laps, only to realise that the water level was particularly low and he couldn't ski straight up onto the beach – so he let go of the rope and gently sank into the water to great applause from us all. Later, Mike Hailwood decided to remove the small bridge over a ditch leading to the bungalow, which resulted in two cars nose diving down into the gap!

Back at the circuit, during practice, the Lucas fuel injection pump and filter gave us some concern as it was supported on a frame behind the front mounted radiator and, with the terrific heat of the day, we thought it could cause trouble. There was some engine misfiring, so we decided after practice to reroute some of the fuel pipes and cover them with asbestos cloth to try and keep them cool.

After another hectic day we returned to our hotel. I was exhausted, so decided to have a well-deserved soak in a lovely deep bath. I ran the water nearly up to the rim and lay back to relax, only for Trevor Taylor to run in and jump into the bath still wearing his race overalls. This caused a waterfall over the side of the bath, onto the floor and into the bedroom. It continued onto the balcony, where it cascaded over the edge onto the sun blind of the room below before dripping gracefully onto the customers enjoying their evening meal on the veranda. Just as well Colin wasn't at this race! It took several towels and quite a while to mop up the mess. I got my own back, when

with some help, we turned over Jimmy and Trevor's room before dragging a naked Trevor out of the bathroom and into the hallway. Jimmy then locked the door, leaving a very embarrassed Trevor running up and down, much to the delight of the housemaids peeping round the corner.

While in South Africa we were looked after by Fred, the local Esso representative. He was a large and jolly chap who always wore shorts at the circuit and was the receiver of many jokes about his hairy legs, which he took in great spirit. But, because of this we began to think that he believed we were all 'gay'! So Trevor decided to pursue this possible line of thinking when he was about to give a speech at the prize giving. Fred was seated alongside him while he praised the race officials, etc... Trevor then began narrating a story about the time he had given a lift to a young man in England and the passenger had twice put his hand on his leg, so he braked hard and asked him to please get out of the car. Before leaving the car the man had squirted perfume on to his suit jacket.

Trevor concluded his story by turning to Fred and said that he was wearing that very suit jacket and asked Fred to smell the sleeve. As the unsuspecting Fred did just that Trevor gave him a kiss and said, "I love you Fred." Poor Fred turned crimson and the whole crowd erupted in laughter. He was a great sport and realised he had been set up!

During the race the cars suffered again with the fuel pump overheating, so unfortunately, we were unable to complete the race. Good old Fred happened to have a few crates of beer and champagne, and very soon we and a few fellow mechanics along with the drivers were well lubricated!

As we didn't have a truck at the circuit to transport the cars back to the garage we had to drive them, but because of the fuel problems they had to be towed. This we did behind the driver's hire cars. I was towed back in Jimmy's car, while he was driving his Galaxie and forgetting that I was on the back. This led to a very hair-raising and sobering ride.

We flew down to East London, while the cars went by truck. Jimmy, Paddy Driver, Mike Hailwood and Sir John Whitmore all hired powerful Benelli motorbikes and had great fun going off road through the bush. All arrived safely, I'm pleased to say.

The race was on December 28th, so we had Christmas at our hotel by the beach where there was a small zoo with penguins in. The sand was so hot you couldn't walk on it. It was a strange way for us to spend the festive period away from our families. There was a nice swimming pool, but it was only three feet deep, with a large notice informing people not to dive in. Most of us took note of this but not Sir John, who climbed onto a table and dived off straight into the pool, splitting his head open and turning the air blue and the pool red!

We drove the cars from the garage to the circuit pit area along the coast road in the morning heat. I was in Jimmy's car and the spectators lining the route were all shouting out "Jim Clark!" This made me quite proud, if not a little embarrassed. These were all black South Africans as apartheid was still very much active in those days, so the black and white communities were separated even at the circuit where there were separate gates and toilets for them.

The race distance was 85 laps (207 miles) and there were over 50,000 spectators spread around the very hot and windy circuit. By the end of the race Jimmy was a minute ahead of Dan Gurney, who was the only other driver on the same lap. What an incredible achievement. Jimmy won seven out of the nine Grands Prix that year and was crowned world champion for the first time, with Graham Hill in the BRM in second place.

The previous year (1962), Chapman said he would give all team members a Mini if we won the world championship. Unfortunately, in the last race in South Africa Graham Hill had beaten Jimmy to the title after Jimmy had retired when an oil gallery plug had come out. Generously, Colin said the offer was still there if we

won the title in 1963. When the Ford Motor Company heard of Colin's offer they vetoed it, and offered Cortina GTs instead! By then, Lotus and Ford were closely linked via the Indianapolis project. Myself, Jim Endruweit (Chief Mechanic), Dick Scammell, Cedric Selzer, David Lazenby, Colin Riley and Ted Woodley all received – in the colour of our choice – a Cortina GT, as promised. They turned up one day on a car transporter and were given to us without ceremony, which was surprising as we thought Ford would want to publicise the fact that they had provided them. These were a much-appreciated gift after working day and night to achieve the coveted championship. A great finish to a great year.

Also, while working on the F1 team, we were fortunate to be given other gifts from other companies. Esso – who can forget the Tiger in the Tank slogan – our early sponsors and probably one the first in motorsport, gave us all electric shavers. A knitting firm gave us all green and yellow striped jumpers. The GPDA sent us all inscribed tankards in appreciation of our 1963 success and Jimmy gave us Enicar Sherpa watches inscribed 'In appreciation of 1963 World Championship, Jim Clark'.

The watch presented to me by Jimmy for my part in his championship success. It's looking a bit scratched but the inscription is still clear.

At the Zonda circuit, I'm doing all the work, while Jackie (in shorts), Tony Rudlin (hat), and Mo Nunn, follow. Our transporter is in the background.

Courtesy of Jackie Oliver.

ARGENTINA – Temporada Series

The 1968 series held in December was the first for Formula Two cars and would consist of four races at three circuits. The first and last at the Buenos Aires Autodrome, with Cordoba and Zonda (San Juan) in between. The great Juan-Manuel Fangio was part of the organising group, it was sponsored by the fuel company, Y.P.F., and with all the leading F2 competitors invited it was a great way to end the season.

I was to be mechanic to Jackie Oliver, who would campaign the Herts and Essex Aero Club Lotus 48, which I spent a considerable time preparing. We were running on a very tight budget, so we had to borrow a spare Cosworth FVA engine just in case we had problems with our own. We didn't really want to use it as we would have had to pay for an overhaul.

Having taken the small Ford Transit transporter with car and equipment down to Tilbury Docks to be shipped out to Argentina, myself, along with Jackie, Tony Rudlin (Team Manager), and another mechanic, Morris (Mo) Nunn – who was still racing himself, but later found fame

creating Ensign racing cars – all flew out from Heathrow on a Pan Am Airlines Boeing 707.

We stepped off the plane in Buenos Aires and were amazed by the searing heat. We had to have two fans on full power in our hotel room at night to help us get some sleep. When the ship arrived we went to the docks to collect the transporter, which had to be craned out of the hold (no drive on and off in those days). We were asked to go on board the freighter and help to move the Matra transporter, which was perched on hundreds of steel tubes and holding up the unloading as no one knew how to start it up. Being a French truck, we couldn't figure it out either, so in the end we had to manhandle it to the main unloading hatch.

The Buenos Aires Autodrome was an interesting circuit as it could be made into many configurations. Some of the cars were hired out to the local Argentinian drivers and every time one of them went past the pit area there was a standing ovation from the crowd in the stands opposite, whether they were being overtaken or on their own.

Between practice sessions it was so warm that we had to put the cars into the garages, or they became so hot it

Our transporter being hoisted off the boat on arrival in Argentina.

> **We stepped off the plane in Buenos Aires and were amazed by the searing heat. We had to have two fans on full power in our hotel room at night to help us get some sleep. When the ship arrived we went to the docks to collect the transporter, which had to be craned out of the hold (no drive on and off in those days).**

was impossible to touch them or pick up your spanners – incredible! Also, the aluminium rear wing would deform with the heat. We would work in swimming trunks for five minutes before showering and continuing. Theft was a common problem in the pits, so all equipment had to be guarded and not left out.

On race day the local fire brigade came to hose down the crowds to keep them cool, and once again when the drivers paraded in front of the stands. The Argentinian ones received tremendous applause, which created a great atmosphere.

> " On race day the local fire brigade came to hose down the crowds to keep them cool, and once again when the drivers paraded in front of the stands. The Argentinian ones received tremendous applause, which created a great atmosphere. "

All the cars were lined up on the grid for the start, so when Jackie gave me the nod to say that his engine had started I walked to the back of the field for safety. There were no Armco barriers protecting the pit lane and I had seen many startline shunts in the past. As soon as the flag was dropped by Fangio, Jochen Rindt was off down the straight from pole position and on to victory.

The Brabham of Piers Courage accelerated forward into the back of the Ferrari of Andrea de Adamich, sending him straight into the wall of the Ferrari pits. Andrea was furiously trying to engage reverse gear, which he did before speeding off down the track, leaving a smoke and water trail that caused him to retire.

Meanwhile, I was running back to our pit ready to start signalling when a large person suddenly landed on the pit lane in front of me. He was a Swiss photographer who had unfortunately been in the wrong place at the wrong time and had been thrown into the air by the rear wheel of de Adamich's Ferrari. Being a dedicated mechanic, I ignored him and carried on to collect my signalling board.

The ambulance in the disguise of a Chevrolet van was summoned, complete with two medics standing on the running boards, wearing white coats with a red cross on. They jumped off, opened the van doors, collected a stretcher and popped the photographer on it before putting him in the rear of the van and speeding off down the pit lane towards the exit gate, which was controlled by soldiers. Unbeknown to the ambulance driver the rear doors had opened and he had lost his patient, who was now laying prone on the pit lane again. The soldiers attempted to wave the driver down, who was gesticulating madly to them to open the gate. When he realised why they hadn't opened the gates he sent the two medics running back to collect the poor patient, but this time minus the stretcher. They picked him up by his arms and legs and ran back to the van. Finally, he was on his way to receive medical care – probably very worried by now. The crowd thought the display was great entertainment and I still managed to collect my board to signal to Jackie, who was oblivious to the 'side show'. The well-known British entertainer, Brian Rix, couldn't have written a better farce.

A footnote to this race was Ferrari's sudden increase in speed compared with previous races in Europe. The engines were supposed to be the same – a V6 Fiat – but it was thought they had changed to a Ferrari V6. The scrutineering was a joke and no protest was lodged.

For the race in Cordoba we all stayed in a nearby hotel. The cars had been prepared and, having been told that we would be informed when we could go through the process of scrutineering before practice, we decided to relax by the hotel pool for a while. We were all in a jovial mood when, suddenly, the sound of racing cars on the circuit could be heard. We rushed off to see what was happening only to

Working on Jackie's type 48 in the sweltering conditions.

find that the Argentinian drivers were getting in some extra practice laps. We then decided to join them – as I said, scrutineering was lax to say the least.

The third race was at Zonda in the San Juan mountainous region. The weather was so hot and we, being the poor relations, had no air conditioning in our small, cramped Transit. The plastic drink cups deformed as they stood on the dashboard and even at speed the air was burning our arms as it came through the window. We asked Fangio if he would be prepared to arrange a flight for us, which he very kindly did, and also offered to have one of his men drive our transporter to the circuit.

The circuit was in a bowl surrounded by barren mountains and had been newly built in a figure of eight shape with a flyover. We had been previously warned that an extremely strong wind called the Zonda could affect the racing.

The first practice went well but was minus Jochen Rindt, who had been joined by his wife, Nina; they decided to miss practice and go to the coast. The next day, the sky blackened and the wind started to blow all the advertisement banners about, blowing sand across the circuit which caused our eyes to sting. It became so bad that it was virtually impossible to go out, so we all retreated to the garages.

Jochen had now arrived back from his jaunt and had to put in a practice time before being allowed to race. He drove off around the sand ridden circuit in an attempt to familiarise himself with it and attempt a time. He managed two laps as we heard him constantly lifting off as it was an impossible task even to see. When he arrived back to the pits his team had to completely strip down the car as the sand had got into all the engine and suspension, also ruining his visor and helmet, which had been sand blasted. His mechanics were not happy as they had to work all night to rebuild it to enable him to start in last place. This did create a spectacular race as he fought his way through

Two of our main rivals, Jonathan Williams and Piers Courage, in a light-hearted mood, as usual.

the field, learning the circuit as he went. A strange sight amongst the spectators was a Jeep with a puma sitting on the bonnet. Hopefully it enjoyed the race!

The final race was back in Buenos Aires, but we had some time out first and stayed in a hotel in the countryside where we swam often and tried to relax. Tony Rudlin decided to arrange for a horse to be delivered to the hotel for us all to experience horse riding. He was a proficient horseman, having taken a bet to learn to ride and complete the journey from London to York on horseback dressed as highwayman Dick Turpin, staying at coaching inns on the way. He was assisted by the RSPCA, who monitored the welfare of the several horses used throughout. He completed the trip but took all the skin off the inside of his legs.

When the horse arrived, Tony jumped on and charged off over dusty fields and hedges. Mo Nunn refused to have a go and when it was my turn the horse refused to budge, even after kicking and cajoling it, so I gave up on one

horsepower! I dismounted, enabling Tony to charge off for the rest of the afternoon.

While driving around in our hire car it was interesting to observe that all the bumpers on the cars were fitted at the same height, so enabling drivers when finding a small parking space to nudge their way in by driving forward and backward, bumping the other cars, who only used a small application of their handbrakes. This practice would also be used at traffic lights if someone stalled to ease them away.

Mo Nunn was driving one evening and said that he was going to race the car next to us at the traffic lights. We persuaded him that it wasn't a good idea as just down the road were two policemen leaning across the boot of a police car, brandishing firearms. Mo was always up for a laugh, but not this time!

Out in the country a good method of slowing vehicles down at crossroads was to have concrete lumps the size of half shaped footballs across the road, which if taken at speed would rip out the underneath of a car. It was a crude but efficient method.

The food was very good, especially the steaks, that we would eat in a small restaurant by the River Plate – where the Germans scuttled one of their battleships (the *Graf Spee*) in World War Two. We were often joined by others who were working or involved with the series. One lunchtime, after a few glasses of the local wine, Mo Nunn got an ice cream cornet and stuck it on top of motoring journalist Andrew Marriott's head, much to everyone's amusement.

Speaking of ice cream there was a vendor at the circuit who would call out "Elardos, elardos!", which we thought meant 'ice cream', so when he was at the other end of the pit lane we would all shout "Elardos, elardos!" and he would rush backwards and forwards thinking he had a competitor!

When it was all over we headed off back home, having enjoyed the experience, and the sunny weather in December!

The Bedford transporter loaded up at Cheshunt.
The smaller Ford 'PMT' version is alongside.

On the way to Monaco in 1962. On board are a type 25, two type 24s and
five mechanics. On a trailer borrowed from Peter Warr is a new type 24
rolling chassis for Filipinetti Racing to be raced by Jo Siffert.

4

LOTUS TRANSPORT

As I have written about the circuits I think it fitting to dedicate a small chapter about the various forms of transport we used.

The main vehicle was our Bedford transporter capable of carrying three F1 cars, spares, toolboxes and up to five mechanics with luggage. It was painted in the Lotus colours of dark green with a yellow stripe. To load the cars we had to open the large tailgate, which once down formed part of the ramp. We then lowered the top ramp down to enable us to push one car forward over the cab and then another behind it. The ramp was then hand wound up into position and a large bar put underneath to hold it in place. The third car then went underneath with spares, etc... which could be accessed via two large side hatches. We then had to crawl in to be able to strap the cars securely for transporting.

The cab consisted of a double seat next to the driver's, with two bunks behind. The top one could be lowered down to provide more seating area. The proximity of the seats meant that we could change drivers without stopping by the driver sliding out to the right and into the back while the next in line would quickly take over the wheel, thus saving valuable minutes. This reminds me of an incident involving Ted Woodley, who was in his forties and the eldest member of the team during my time. He was driving at night through France in thick fog, saying he was okay to carry on after his two-hour stint. He was obviously tired and followed the edge of the road into a garage forecourt, before nodding off at the wheel. David Lazenby jumped out of the cab and shone a torch light through the windscreen onto Ted's face while we all shouted "Look out Ted!" He woke up thinking he was having a head on collision, and this nearly caused him to have a heart attack – a foolish thing to do and not repeated. The standard two-hour driving time was then made compulsory. Lunch was taken at cafés on route and we usually sampled the local wine, but the rule was that the next two drivers weren't allowed this pleasure.

David Lazenby could sleep for ten hours at a time and nothing would wake him. This was proved on the occasion we were driving on the continent in good weather and we had all the windows open. Unfortunately, we hit a roadside sign, shattering our wing mirror and showering the sleeping Laz's face with glass. This didn't disturb him at all and we had brushed off all the glass before he awoke.

Driving over the French Alps the Bedford's brakes began to overheat and fade, so we had to pull into a lay-by for them to cool off. With vertical drops and hairpin bends it would have been unsafe to go on. We all climbed out and sat by the side of the road. Laz fell asleep again, so we covered him with a blanket and made a cross out of some tape and placed it by his head. The surprised look from passing motorists and a scooter driver, who looked back and nearly fell off, caused us all to chuckle.

On a similar journey travelling over the Alps at night we heard a creaking noise from the front area of the cab. The

driver's door was above the front wheel, so when getting
out you put your foot on the wheel nuts. On this occasion,
one fell off. We'd had a lucky escape, as on inspection we
found the others were loose. I always enjoyed driving on
these mountain roads, and when on the descent would
sometimes accelerate between the hairpins, much to the
annoyance of Dick Scammell, who would (rightfully)
reprimand me.

We always had a very tight schedule, which meant
driving as fast as possible, much to the anger of foreign
truckers, who had to drive in line up steep hills; but as our
vehicle was lighter and quicker we passed them all so didn't
queue in line at the customs post, much to their annoyance.

While travelling back from Monza, over the Mont
Cenis Pass, we noticed a lovely ski lodge high up on the
mountain and commented that it would be a nice place
for a holiday. Shortly afterwards we took a wrong turning
and started to climb up the pass through the snow.
Unable to turn around on the narrow road with banks of
snow on either side, we eventually found ourselves at the
aforementioned ski lodge.

The auto route from Ostend to Brussels, known as the
Jabbeke Road, was an inviting long stretch of three lane
motorway which gave us the opportunity for a competition
to see who could drive its entire length without lifting off
the throttle. It wasn't easy, especially with the traffic, so we
never managed it, unfortunately.

It was possible to change the rear axle ratio with a
switch in the cab, which allowed us to have eight gears
and enabled us to get up to a reasonable 80mph. But, we

In the car park at Cheshunt is Peter Warr's type 22 that he took to the races on his aforementioned trailer until... That's Tesco's headquarters opposite. I wonder what happened to them?

were outdone by Rob Walker's transporter, which was the quickest. Rob's mechanics, Alf Francis and Tony Cleverley, drove the noisy, supercharged, flat-four two-stroke Commer with great gusto. BRM's Leyland Tiger was also quite fast. It was always an exciting race to see who would get back to the ferry first. We would race each other while passing beers to each other through the cab windows.

Once back at the workshops, we would literally rip out the engines as quickly as possible, leaving oil and debris over the floor. They were then loaded into the van to charge up to Coventry Climax in the hope of being first to have our engines rebuilt, as most teams used the Climax engine and they were worked on on a first come first served basis. After the long trip home we were all tired, so the mechanic to drive the van was chosen by the short straw method, while the other lucky ones were able to go home for a much needed rest.

On one such trip, having drawn the shortest straw, I found myself following a bread van along a narrow country lane in Hertfordshire. A police motorcyclist came towards us waving us into the side of the road as a large lorry carrying concrete beams was heading our way. As it passed one of the overhanging beams tore the side out of the bread van, scattering bread and cakes over the road before continuing without stopping. This resulted in me having to make a statement on behalf of the bread van driver as I was a witness to the event, which made me very late in reaching Coventry.

In 1962, we had to take a customer car to Monaco for the Swiss driver, Jo Siffert, which meant towing a trailer behind the transporter. We borrowed a trailer from Peter Warr, which he used to transport his Lotus 22 and 23. Peter said whatever you do, make sure you tow it with a car on at all times, as if it bounced around empty it would fall to pieces. After the Grand Prix, Jo took his car back to Switzerland while we headed for home, making sure we put a team car on the trailer.

Somewhere in the middle of France we heard a strange grinding noise, which upon investigation was the trailer being dragged along having shed one of its wheels. It was totally irreparable, so we loaded the car into the transporter and threw the trailer into the ditch. Poor Peter was less than pleased when we broke the news, but Colin did replace it with a new one.

Our other means of transport was the famous 'PMT', which is mentioned in the following chapter covering my adventures in Europe, particularly those in Sicily.

Trevor Taylor's car in the paddock at Solitude beside our Bedford transporter. Jim Bull, our gearbox mechanic, about to get to work.

With Jim Endruweit (left) and Cedric Selzer (right). It looks as if Jim is regaling us with one of his many tales.

> "We once took our Bedford transporter for a lap of the circuit, although negotiating the Karussell was a bit tricky!"

5

CIRCUIT TALES – PART TWO
EUROPE

SOLITUDE

Situated in a hilly, forested area close to Stuttgart, the circuit was named after the nearby Solitude Castle. It was a road circuit lined with trees and had no safety barriers. The circuit was originally used for motorcycle racing, but F1 races were held between 1961 and 1965. Also, Mercedes and Porsche used it for testing.

> *It was a road circuit lined with trees and had no safety barriers.*

In 1963, for the non-championship race we took three works Lotus 25s for Jimmy, Trevor and Peter Arundell. Jimmy's car had the new Colin Chapman designed lightweight driveshafts fitted, but at the start of the race under acceleration they twisted up. Cedric Selzer and I quickly replaced the shafts with the older and well raced type. Jimmy then went out again to demonstrate his talent and set many fastest laps, but only managed to complete 17 of the 25 lap race distance. Peter finished in second place while Trevor retired with final drive problems.

I returned in 2008 and the control tower was still there along with the pits, which were in good repair and being used. From there, we went on to the Mercedes Museum at Stuttgart, which was absolutely incredible.

NÜRBURGRING

The ultimate test; 14 miles of jumps, bumps, blind crests, every conceivable type of corner: fast, slow and blind. All lined by trees; no safety barriers, negotiated in around nine minutes if the circuit was dry for its entire length, which wasn't always the case. The undulating nature would cause some drivers to feel quite unwell, something I witnessed first-hand when Jackie Oliver was violently sick when racing the F2 car. No wonder it was later termed 'The Green Hell'.

With such a long lap the Grand Prix would be 'only' 14/15 laps (over 200 miles), so us mechanics had plenty of time to wander – usually during practice – down the pit road and chat to other teams. In my case, that was until I missed giving Jimmy the signal board, making me none too popular with A.C.B. Chapman.

Many of the drivers would arrive a few days before the race and hire a road car to learn the circuit. This usually resulted in the more experienced putting in fast times. In 1967, Jimmy lapped in a time of 8 minutes 4.1 seconds in a road car, which was 12 seconds faster than Denny Hulme in his Brabham-Repco. We once took our Bedford transporter for a lap of the circuit, although negotiating the Karussell was a bit tricky!

The restaurant was just opposite the pit area, so after

we had arrived and unloaded the cars into our allotted garage we popped across for a coffee. While there on one occasion a white Mercedes roared by occupied by Dan Gurney, Phil Hill and Richie Ginther. They were checking out the circuit but two laps later they came into the restaurant looking rather sheepish. Apparently, one was steering while the other was changing gear, but they got it all wrong and spun it. This must have been quite frightening due to the narrowness of the circuit and close proximity of the trees and drop offs.

In 1962, after first practice, Mercedes brought out their W154 Grand Prix car from 1939. It was brought on an old Mercedes open-backed truck with a canvas covered rear, which was all in keeping with the car. It ran on some special fuel, which resulted in streaming eyes if you stood

behind it. Hermann Lang climbed in and put on a white leather helmet (I noticed that he had enormous hands) and set off to lap the circuit. All the Formula One drivers were amused by this huge silver car and went to the pit wall to see him pass, which he did at tremendous speed and changed into top gear as he did so. He then had to brake extremely hard for the hairpin and only just made it around. We were all amazed and it was a real treat for all of us. I have since seen this beautiful car again, but this time it was on display in the incredible Mercedes Museum in Stuttgart. The original location for the museum – then much smaller – was near the entrance to the circuit.

There were many incidents and one that stands out involved Peter Arundell. He recalled, while driving one of the works Elans, a hairy moment in one of the corners

The Mercedes W154 before Hermann Lang gave the car a demonstration run to remember.

used on the cars) with the dreaded oxy-acetylene. Then, from the Lucas truck we scrounged a long length of wire which was connected to the inner tube and buried it out of sight in the bikers' paddock. Next time they were revving up their engines we ignited the inner tube, which sent loads of grass and earth flying high up into the air!

The 1964 race saw an influx of Japanese mechanics, complete with their white work gloves. Honda had arrived and the car was to be driven by the American, Ronnie Bucknum. Night time saw us working very late and eating our standard allowance of sandwiches 'on the hoof' as there was no time to stop. The Japanese contingent had waiter service from the restaurant to bring a meal across and they proceeded to sit down in amongst a car that was in several pieces to dine. Their job lists were of course in Japanese and covered many blackboards. The Honda engine was a work of art (apart from the Coke can used as a catch tank on the gearbox) and it impressed us all. Bucknum was last on the grid and one minute adrift of the pole position time of John Surtees but went well in the race until he spun off at the Karussell.

After practice, the public were allowed onto the circuit with their cars for a fee of ten Deutsche Marks per lap. Away went various Porsches, Mercedes, Renaults, even some Citroën 2CVs, racing round the track. Approximately ten minutes later away would go the fire brigade, ambulance and breakdown trucks to recover – three at a time – many of the fine machines that had come to a sad end.

When leaving the circuit you had to complete a 90 degree turn to get back onto the road. I was driving our Bedford transporter and noticed a policeman standing on a round wooden box from where he was directing the traffic. He wanted me to go round his box but I didn't have the steering lock to be able to, so I gesticulated that I should pass in front of him – but he insisted that I drove around his box. He was to regret that decision as, when I tried to do the impossible, I crushed his box causing him

that ended with him upside down in the middle of the track, unable to remove his seatbelt and being soaked in petrol. He looked one way to see a corner, which would taken by a car at any time, and the other to see a German soldier (they helped out at meetings) running towards him with a glowing cigarette! Fortunately, all ended well and he was unscathed apart from his pride and the car.

We often had to work all night, which led to another incident. A motorcycle race was also on the programme and the riders/mechanics were all camping in a grass paddock behind our garage. They appeared to be 'partying' and running up their incredibly noisy two-stroke engines at 6am, which was really annoying us, so it was decided to deal with the matter. While the riders and crews were out practising we inflated an inner tube (currently

Colin's plane at Heathrow after being flown back by Cedric.

G·ARYV

to make a quick leap to safety. He was not amused and blew his whistle furiously, but I was unable to stop as there was a long line of vehicles behind me. After a few yards we passed a stationary police car. The occupants were laughing and gave us the thumbs up!

The most memorable non-racing highlight of our many trips was when Phil Hill took three of us for a ride around the circuit in his Alfa Romeo saloon car. He knew the track better than most due to competing in the endurance races for Ferrari, as well as in Formula One. The most exhilarating part was the Karussell, where the track dived down right into a bowl then out over the top. We all had to put our hands on the inside of the roof to keep us in our seats, as the car was leaping and bouncing along, with Phil driving one handed, while casually relating to us who went off and where! An unforgettable experience.

After one of the races, Graham Hill, Cedric Selzer and myself were offered a lift back to England in Colin Chapman's plane. This was great as we would be back well before the transporter, giving us the luxury of two days off. We headed off at great speed to the military aerodrome where Colin had been given permission to

land. This was an ex-Luftwaffe aerodrome and there were American-built Starfighters parked either side of the runway. Apparently, they were grounded due to ejector seat maintenance problems.

As we picked up speed down the runway Colin says to Cedric, "You are learning to fly aren't you?" and immediately handed him the controls. Cedric flew back to the UK, with Colin taking over just as we approached Heathrow. The landing was equally as exhilarating as Colin opened a map of the airport on his lap and was being given numerous instructions from the Control Tower as to which runway to take immediately after touchdown because we were being followed by a Boeing 707! Sure enough, just after we turned off the main runway the 707 thundered by.

Colin then dashed to catch a flight to America, while the three of us shared a taxi back home to Hampstead, dropping Graham off at his home in Mill Hill, where he was greeted by his wife Bette and young son, Damon. Little did we know then that he was to follow his father into motor racing and emulate him in becoming world champion, the only father and son to achieve such a feat.

HOCKENHEIM

Hockenheim is in a picturesque forest area of Germany, located near to the Rhine and the town of Speyer. It is, of course, synonymous with the death of Jim Clark.

It has been well documented over the years as to what caused Jim's accident. Despite a full investigation carried out at RAF Farnborough proving inconclusive, the general feeling is that a rear tyre punctured at high-speed, pitching the car off into the trees – no Armco or straw bales then – giving Jim no chance of survival. The car's remains were picked up by his mechanic, 'Beaky' Sims, marshals, spectators and Graham Hill, who had stopped to help. I wasn't at the meeting but did the F2 races in June and October that year with Jackie Oliver in a Lotus 48, the type Jim lost his life in. At the June meeting the Australian driver Frank Gardner, who was quite a character and comedian, commented when sat at the back of the field that they should reverse the grid to give him a better chance!

A memorial was erected in Jim's honour near to the accident site and has in recent years been renovated and moved – due to extensive changes to the circuit that cut out that section – to a more fitting place for people to see and pay their respects to one of the greatest drivers of all time. I visited the circuit a few years ago to pay my own personal tribute. My wife, Shirley, had made arrangements with the Circuit Manager to allow us to walk to the forest area where Jim lost his life. A sad moment.

The circuit itself wasn't very challenging. It was basically two long straights, one of which was slightly curved, and a series of corners near to the start/finish area. This section was known as the 'Stadium', due to it being lined by huge grandstands. The long straights provided many opportunities for slipstreaming. Jackie Oliver once said that he could pick up a tow from about 100 yards without even seeing the car in front and could feel the hole in the air helping the car along. This created some spectacular racing with a bunch of cars dicing, often with the last in the bunch appearing on the following lap at the head of the pack. This was especially important on the last lap. If you were able to enter the Stadium section in front, you would be able to hold everyone off. This was all thought out by the driver, with no technical assistance and just a pit board for communication.

My off-track memories are mainly centered around using the hotel swimming pool with some of the drivers and consuming far too much of the local wine in the evening after F2 practice with all the other mechanics.

ZANDVOORT

Situated in sand dunes, and close to the seaside town that gave the circuit its name, the location and surroundings caused many problems; the obvious being sand blown onto the circuit resulting in a constant change in grip levels.

The teams and cars were based in various garages in the town and would be driven the short distance to the circuit, while we walked. I remember our garage having large, distinctive stone tiles.

Our hotel – also host to most of the drivers and mechanics – was a magnificent building with some rooms overlooking the beach and the woven basket-type seats for the holidaymakers to relax in. We never had time to relax or sample the beach! The roof of the main dining area was supported by huge columns. Innes Ireland, with much military experience, wrapped his arms and legs around one of these columns and climbed up to the roof and removed a light bulb, much to the amusement of all concerned. Not to be outdone by Lotus, Graham Hill – then driving for BRM – tried to do the same but fell down onto one of the long tables to great applause and laughter, after only climbing a few feet.

Other non-hotel, pre-race entertainment was provided

on one occasion by a DAF-powered Heineken airship in the shape of a beer barrel. It was supported by an aeroplane towing a banner with 'Durex' written on it. Although this caused a smile amongst the British contingent it was actually advertising a Dutch brand of sticky tape similar to our Sellotape. Another amusing event was when Stirling Moss, unwittingly, sat in the back of a small Simca saloon car, and was then driven around the track on two wheels by a stunt driver.

Unfortunately, not all memories are happy ones. In 1968, when I was running the semi-works Herts and Essex Aero Club Lotus 48 for Jackie Oliver in F2, the meeting was marred when Chris Lambert in a Brabham tangled with Clay Regazzoni in a Tecno. Chris went across the grass and hit a straw bale, which had been placed in front of the Armco barrier. This launched him onto the top of the barrier (we could see his ring gear marks on top of the Armco), and flying head-on into the banking at the side of the vehicle access tunnel under the circuit. He died instantly. His mechanic at the time was Alistair Dimock, who had previously worked with us at Lotus. A sad occasion.

Being a Lotus mechanic was often full of surprises. One such time was in 1962, when I suddenly found myself on the way to Zandvoort instead of my bed! We had all been preparing the revolutionary Lotus 25 for its debut appearance. The 25 was, of course, the first F1 car to have an aluminium monocoque. An early drawback was the fuel bags located in the side pontoons either side of the driver. Without the knowledge of foam filling, as the car braked the fuel would rush forward and load up the front suspension quite heavily.

Anyway, I'm digressing. The car was still being finished as the team transporter left Cheshunt with the two spaceframe Type 24s bound for Zandvoort. We worked all night and, by midday on the following day, the 25 was loaded onto our fast pick-up truck, known to us all as 'PMT' because of its number plate, and also its temperamental reputation!

I look to be enjoying myself in the 25, which was fitted with a long-range fuel tank for Zandvoort.

We were all in our once white, but now rather grey overalls, with red eyes, beard stubble and absolutely knackered. I was waving goodbye to the two other mechanics and wishing them good luck before heading back home for a well-earned sleep, when A.C.B.C. said, "What are you doing waving goodbye? – you are going." I mentioned that I had no clothes, no money and, more importantly, no passport. "Don't worry, we will sort it out" he replied. Without time to even ring home, we rushed to Southend airport to fly the car over to Holland on a Silver City car transport plane.

On arrival I was marched off to the customs building, where I tried to explain my situation, but was told to send for my passport immediately. When I told Chapman of my predicament his reply was, "Oh don't bother about that, the car is the most important thing." He gave me some money to purchase clean clothes and then the transporter arrived to take us to Zandvoort, where once again we started to work on the car.

There were some problems with the 5-speed synchromesh ZF gearbox that I looked after, so I ended up working most of the night to fix the problems. At one stage I even spent time in the hotel kitchen heating gears in the oven! The chef gave me strawberries and cream while we waited for the gears to 'cook'.

The 25 proved to be very quick on its first outing but, unfortunately, Jimmy could only manage ninth position – mainly due to the continuing gearbox problems, which had proved troublesome to fix.

A well-known incident occurred before the start of the Grand Prix. Jimmy and Dan Gurney were sat on the grass with some other drivers watching the saloon car race when the Dutch police (not renowned for their politeness) arrived and told Jimmy and Dan to move. They recognised Dan but not Jimmy, and asked Dan who the other person was? To which Dan replied that he had no idea! So Jim was marched off down the pit lane – much to Dan's amusement – until it was pointed out who they had captured.

It wasn't only the drivers that fell foul of the Dutch police. Colin's wife, Hazel, and Jimmy's girlfriend, Sally Stokes, found themselves in trouble when they sat on the roof of the pits for a bird's eye view. The police arrived and insisted that they came down. At the end of the race, Jimmy was surrounded by mounted police to keep the crowd back.

Even Colin found himself in trouble when he was involved in a scuffle with Dutch police after being told that he was wearing his pit pass in the wrong place (on his belt and not his right arm). He pointed out – not in the politest way – that he would wear it where he wanted, and then threw a punch. The police were not amused (unsurprisingly) and, once the race had finished, Colin was taken away for a short stay in the cells.

After the race we were all obliged to return to the hotel and attend the prize giving ceremonies, which included drivers from the other races receiving their awards as well. The ceremonies were conducted in Dutch and usually lasted over an hour, with many speeches by the organising body. To counteract the boredom we had a bet amongst ourselves, as to which speaker could talk the longest. When it was all over, we loaded up the cars and set off back to England in the transporter. I was still without my passport, so had to hide under the bunk in the back. It was a very uncomfortable journey back home.

REIMS

We all enjoyed this French road circuit situated in the region known for its champagne. The track was very uninspiring due to its layout consisting of three long straights and three corners, one of which was a tight hairpin. Almost the entire race would be a slipstreaming battle and was usually run in extremely hot conditions. At over 50 laps (approx. 270 miles) it was a real test of stamina.

Some of the overtaking took place in the pit lane, as there were no barriers or straw bales. When you were signalling your driver you had to be prepared to beat a hasty retreat over the pit wall.

Toto Roche – a real character – was the Clerk of the Course and the official starter. He was a short, round man, who usually stood in front of the pole position car before dropping the Tricolour flag and running – if you could call it that! – to safety.

Our cars were prepared at the local Citroën garage in the town, while the other teams were also located in nearby garages. The mechanics had to drive the F1 cars to the circuit through the town, contending with traffic lights and tram lines en route, as well as the local 'racers' wanting to race us. It was great fun lining up at the traffic lights with a row of French would be racing drivers in their Citroëns and Peugeots.

Some of the overtaking took place in the pit lane, as there were no barriers or straw bales. When you were signalling your driver you had to be prepared to beat a hasty retreat over the pit wall.

On one occasion after arriving back at the garage to prepare Jimmy's car – as per the gov's job list – the man himself decided (for once) to put on some overalls and assist us, but asked us to check everything he did. This became rather annoying so Cedric said to him, "F*** off Chapman and let us get on with it." Amazingly, Colin walked off and, even more amazingly, Cedric kept his job.

Occasionally, Colin wasn't present as he suffered badly with hay fever and had to stay in the hotel, which was good for us as there was less hassle. One year after attending practice he fled back to his hotel in a rented Citroën, and as usual, he was driving too fast and soon had the local gendarmes in hot pursuit. He managed to outfumble them and, after covering the car with a white sheet, left the car in our garage. Later that night, Innes Ireland asked Colin if he could borrow the car. Colin said yes, and off Innes goes. Of course, Innes knew nothing of Colin's earlier escapade, so ended up having a very embarrassing encounter with the local police.

The Grand Prix was supported by the local champagne companies, who supplied an abundance of bottles for distribution amongst the competitors for fastest lap, pole position and the winner. We came away with a van load of the stuff that I drove through customs. When asked what was in the van I replied, "It's full of champagne." The officer laughed and waved me through without inspection. Sometimes it does pay to tell the truth!

I also worked at Reims when I ran the Herts and Essex Aero Club Lotus 48 Formula 2 car for Jackie Oliver. In the paddock we were next to the Gold Leaf Team Lotus set up, who were running works cars for Jimmy and Graham (Hill). The cars were fitted with Ford FVA engines that had slide throttles, and to get the engine running you had to squirt petrol from an oil squirt can down the intakes while controlling the throttle lever. If the engine spat back (and they usually did) the oil can could catch fire in your hand. If it caught fire, you threw it aside rather quickly. On this occasion, when I threw it away, it rolled under the Team Lotus cars. I have never seen mechanics move so fast. Luckily, I managed to retrieve it before any damage was done.

Another petrol related incident occurred about 15 minutes before the warming-up lap of the F2 race. I was told that petrol was dripping from underneath Jackie's car. At first I thought they were joking, but soon realised they weren't when I noticed one of the two thin rubber fuel tanks had sprung a leak. I ripped out the tank, with fuel spilling everywhere, and managed to get a new one in and fill it up just after the other cars had left the paddock. Much to our disappointment, the officials refused to allow Jackie out to join the other cars. Jackie was in tears, and I was left feeling extremely angry and frustrated.

As in F1, it was just as important in F2 to get a tow off the car ahead and use their slipstream. During practice we noticed that Jochen Rindt in the Winklemann Brabham hadn't come past the pits for several laps, making us all think he must have 'fell off', but, to our surprise, his mechanics seemed unperturbed. With it being a road circuit it had many exits off onto the temporarily closed French roads and Jochen had pulled off onto one of these side roads to wait until all the cars were spread out, whereupon he chased them and got a tow off at least half the field. This enabled him to put in an unbelievable lap time, and secured him pole position with some ease.

Thillois was the last corner, and if you approached it in first place you were almost certain to be slipstreamed and passed before the start/finish line. In one race, Graham Hill was leading approaching Thillois and knew full well what would happen. He slowed down in the hope that he would be overtaken and then he could reverse the position in the run to the flag. He underestimated Jochen, who took to the escape road, which was a triangle-shaped piece of road with grass between it and the circuit. By going the long way round, he managed to gain enough speed to outdrag Graham to the finish, who was certainly outfumbled by Jochen that day.

Another incident I remember at Thillois was when Trevor Taylor in the works Lotus had to pull off the circuit during practice and parked the car about 50ft from the track. The officials wouldn't allow us to retrieve the car as a race was about to start immediately after practice.

Unfortunately, on the last lap of the race the driver in last place spun off the track, across the grass and straight into our 'parked' car, causing a lot of damage. Chapman's comments are not fit to be repeated and it meant another sleepless night repairing the damage.

After the Grand Prix all the drivers and mechanics were invited to the chateau of Louis Chandon (famous champagne magnet) for an evening meal. The driveway was over a mile long and, on arrival, our cars were taken and parked by the staff. The dining room was magnificent, with long oak tables and as much food as you could eat. The champagne waiters, who wore leather caps and long leather aprons, would refill our glasses on a regular basis, making sure they were full throughout the evening. Needless to say, a good time was had by all!

ROUEN-LES-ESSARTS

Situated just outside the medieval city of Rouen, it was an average circuit (in my opinion), that had been used for many years, with some parts being marked out with just straw bales. The meeting was usually started with a French bicycle race.

In 1962, Jimmy secured pole position despite, unfortunately, having a tooth break off the steering rack. The racks hadn't been heat treated correctly, and as many of the cars used the same manufacturer, there was a great deal of activity behind the pits as mechanics dismantled racks and pinions to inspect the teeth for signs of cracking.

Ferrari wasn't present due to a metal workers' strike at the factory. Unfortunately, Jimmy failed to finish due to front suspension problems. The race was won by Dan Gurney in his 8-cylinder Porsche, followed by the Cooper-Climax of Tony Maggs and the BRM of Richie Ginther. A new lap record was set by Graham Hill, who subsequently retired from the race due to fuel injection problems.

Toto Roche was, as at Reims, the flamboyant starter. In 1960, he managed to miss the victorious car of Jack Brabham and failed to give him the chequered flag. He was certainly a one-off. As well as Toto, the drivers also had the gendarmes to contend with. They used to line up either side of the track just after the finish line to keep enthusiastic spectators from running into the pit area. This caused a problem for John Surtees, who was in trouble with no clutch and only fourth gear. When he tried to pull into the pits his way was blocked by the gendarmes. Maurice Trintignant swerved to miss Surtees and was hit at high-speed by Trevor Taylor in our works car. The ensuing collision caused both cars to go off into the bank. Amazingly, no one was hurt, but it brought an immediate end to the lining of the track.

Amongst the other races held were two for Formula Juniors. Both were won by Peter Arundell in his works

Trevor Taylor's car back at Cheshunt showing the damage inflicted in the incident with Trintignant.

Lotus. In one of the Junior races it was a Team Lotus one-two-three, with Alan Rees and Bob Anderson following Peter home.

1964 saw us back again and added to the Grand Prix weekend was the Festival of Speed, comprising of two Formula Three races and a race each for cars from the 'Golden Age', and veteran cars. After practice, Jimmy was offered the opportunity to drive the Honourable Patrick Lindsay's ERA, most commonly known, as 'Remus'. He drove about four laps and passed the pits using the oil hand pump to sustain the oil pressure. He enjoyed the drive tremendously and managed to better Patrick's time on his first timed lap. I wish I'd had the time to take a photograph.

Patrick Lindsay consequently went on to win the race from a Bugatti and a Frazer-Nash. A sad note was when a beautiful French racing blue Talbot was damaged and the driver was in tears as he had taken years to rebuild it.

Before the race, while we were working on the cars in the grass paddock behind the pits, there was a punch up in the café which was just above the pits. This resulted in two large advertising umbrellas being knocked over the rail onto the ground behind our cars. These were placed in our transporter and provided us with shelter for many seasons.

Trevor leading Jimmy around the picturesque streets.

PAU

An attractive town in south west France, and like Monaco a street circuit, but with snowcapped mountains in the distance and no sea!

My first visit was over the Easter weekend in 1963 for a 100 lap (171 miles) non-championship Formula One race. The day before the race there was a motorbike and sidecar event. The build and preparation of these outfits amazed us as they seemed so crude. One of the outfits was that of the Swiss champion, Florian Camathias, who two years later was killed at Brands Hatch and became another racing fatality.

The cars were prepared in the local Renault garage and we had Jimmy and Trevor on the front row for us. The competition was poor so they both promised to make the race look good for the many spectators that had arrived on a lovely sunny day. They were passing and repassing each other and lapped the opposition several times. They promised to call into the pits for a drink of Coke but it didn't happen! Jimmy won, with Trevor a worthy second.

In the F2 race Graham Hill came into the pits rather white-faced and said that he'd just experienced a frightening moment. Unbeknown to him a photographer had moved a bale of straw to stand on. This might sound insignificant, but to Graham it was crucial and nearly caused him to crash as the bale of straw was his braking point, so moving it made him much closer to the corner than he thought and he had to brake at the last minute to avoid a statue in the middle of the road.

I was to return many years with Reine Wisell and GRD for the annual F2 race, but that's another story...

Trevor and Jimmy helping us prepare the cars in the baking hot conditions.

IMOLA

We arrived at Imola the week after the aforementioned Pau meeting. Again, it was a non-championship race over a slightly shorter distance of 156 miles. Jim won again, but this time Trevor finished in ninth place. It was an extremely hot weekend and both drivers helped us prepare the cars.

It was an interesting, twisty circuit surrounded by cream, red tiled houses – typical Italy – that Ferrari used for testing regularly, with it only being about an hour's drive away from the factory. Following the death of Enzo's son, Dino, it was renamed the Autodromo Dino Ferrari. Following Enzo's death in 1988, it was changed to its current name of Autodromo Internazionale Enzo e Dino Ferrari.

During the trip we were invited to visit Scuderia Centro Sud, the race team based near the circuit. In their workshops were numerous Ferrari and Maserati single-seater and sports cars. A Maserati 250F (once raced by Fangio and Moss) had a cockpit so large that my colleagues Ted Woodley and Cedric Selzer both sat in it, with the latter sitting on Ted's lap. The car looked so large compared with the Lotus 25.

In recent times it is, of course, synonymous with Roland Ratzenberger and Ayrton Senna, who both succumbed to their injuries after being involved in huge accidents during the Grand Prix meeting in 1994. They were both great drivers who I knew well from my days at Van Diemen when they were starting out in Formula Ford 1600.

The remains of a Fiat Abarth after contact with the top rail of the barrier on the banking.

MONZA

One of the great and original circuits set in a large park on the outskirts of Milan, which also housed a motor museum and fine restaurants. The large paddock area – which we all considered was excellent to work in – was cobbled and surrounded on two sides by lock up garages painted cream with green woodwork.

My first trip was in 1960 with Jimmy and Innes. We (Team Lotus) always had the latest developed cars, while our customers had the older models. On this occasion, Rob Walker was running a car for Stirling and wanted one of the new cars, so a deal was struck with Chapman for Innes and Stirling to swap cars – much to the disgust of Innes. This meant a quick 'repaint' of Innes' car into the Rob Walker colours of dark blue with a white stripe around the nose. Rob's mechanics, the legendary Alf

Francis and Tony Cleverly, worked all night to complete this task and set the car up for Stirling. Unfortunately, neither finished the race; Innes due to bad handling and Stirling with wheel bearing problems, partly due to the rough surface of the banking.

The famous banking was extremely dangerous due to its uneven surface and loads that put enormous strain through all parts of the car, that you were unable to prepare for due to only encountering such conditions once a year. Also, the layout meant that cars would have to pass the pits twice; firstly, on the standard flat circuit, and then towards the end of the lap they passed closely in front of the pits onto the banking which passed over the first part of the circuit, thus making it two completely different types of driving in one lap. This was very difficult for the drivers to adapt to.

The prize giving was at the local hotel, arranged by the race organisers, the Automobile Club of Milan, and all teams had to attend. These events were usually either hilarious or very boring. The latter if the senior officials of the club gave very long speeches in Italian. Again, to pass the time, we would have a bet amongst ourselves who would speak the longest. Adding to their length was the presentations, which weren't just for the Grand Prix but other local races, at not just Monza, but also other circuits.

By the time we reached the dining hall, having suffered the prize giving, we were all fairly deflated. So, with this in mind, picture the scene – Team Lotus and hangers-on at one end of the huge dining hall, while at the other end was the Cooper team plus hangers-on. To the side of the hall were the BRM contingent and the other teams. In between these formidable groups were innocent Italians having a quiet meal out with their families.

As the wine started to flow so did the jokes and verbal interaction amongst our brethren! Halfway through the meal Colin (Chapman) decided to throw a bun at John Cooper and the BRM group. This action resulted in war breaking out! The respectable diners took cover or left while the waiters were now bringing us ammunition consisting of ice cream and other items. I ended up with my white shirt covered in red wine and one of our new mechanics – the Kiwi, Leo Wybrott – ending up with a black eye, when he popped up from under the table to be attacked by an orange. When it all subsided everyone chipped in to a clean-up fund and drinks for the understanding staff.

We left the hotel rather worse for wear and saw Dan Gurney's Fiat rental car outside. This prompted us into action again and between us we lifted it up and placed it neatly on the rostrum in the middle of the roundabout that the local traffic police used to stand on and elegantly wave their arms about in a vain attempt to control the masses.

Another incident involving a Fiat was when we arrived at the circuit on race day after a late night working. We had a small Fiat hire car, which six of us had managed to squeeze into. We were all wearing our clean Lotus green overalls, making it obvious who we were, but the police stopped us at the gate and asked to see our passes. Unfortunately, Jim Endruweit (Chief Mechanic) had left them in the paddock garage! The armed police started to get irate as we were blocking the road and after an altercation they pulled us out of the Fiat and lined us up by the fence – they also stopped our transporter going through. The BRM and Ferrari mechanics drove straight through, having a good laugh at us. Eventually, they released Jim and he made a mad dash to the paddock to retrieve the passes. A precious hour was lost while the situation was sorted out.

The following year, a hot and sunny Monza saw Ferrari dominant in practice. They took five of the first six places on the grid, with Wolfgang von Trips taking pole position followed by Ricardo Rodriguez, Richie Ginther and Phil Hill filling the top four, while Giancarlo Baghetti was sixth. Graham Hill was the interloper in fifth place. We qualified seventh (Jimmy) and ninth (Innes).

Jimmy made a good start and was behind von Trips. Approaching the Parabolica for the second time, the German Count and Jimmy collided, resulting in the Ferrari flying off the track, up the grass banking and into the wire fence where spectators were watching, until finally ending up in the middle of the circuit alongside Jimmy's car which had spun but remained on the track. David Lazenby and I had started to walk around the inside of the track towards the Parabolica to see if we could find out what had happened to Jimmy. A horrifying sight greeted us, with spectators staggering about covered in blood – it was obvious some were badly injured – while blankets covered those who had died. When we saw the cars in the distance we began to realise what had happened. In total, 15 spectators lost their lives along with von Trips. Unbelievably, the race continued and was won by Phil Hill, who became world champion – the first American to do so. Only Phil and von Trips had been in contention, so a terribly sad way for the American to claim the crown.

In Italian law, after an accident, members of the team are held responsible – so we were not allowed to continue to our next race at Zeltweg in Austria. The cars of Jimmy and von Trips were locked in the paddock garages with a policeman on guard. Colin and Jimmy had been advised by a solicitor to fly back to England immediately, leaving us mechanics to face the music. That evening at our hotel we saw the accident shown many times on Italian television.

The next day we went back to the circuit and asked the police officers to open the garage so we could examine the car, but were told that was not possible, so we prepared the other car in readiness for practice in Austria, should we be allowed to leave Italy.

> "*The next day we went back to the circuit and asked the police officers to open the garage so we could examine the car, but were told that was not possible, so we prepared the other car in readiness for practice in Austria, should we be allowed to leave Italy.*"

Before leaving I decided to take a closer look at the infamous banking and hopped over the fence to climb up it. I had to scramble up to the top on all fours as it was extremely steep. While I was hanging on precariously to the top safety rail I heard an engine start up. Luckily for me, I let go of the rail and tumbled down the banking just in time to scramble over the fence as the BRM of Graham Hill roared by. He was doing a few laps before leaving for Austria.

Having examined this concrete banking at close hand it gave answers to a few questions regarding the handling of the car. The concrete was in a bad condition, with many cracks and signs of breaking up. This, along with the G-forces, was bending the suspension rocking arms and was the reason why the cars were needing ride height adjustments. Many of the drivers said that the increase in G-force made the car difficult to handle and, when changing gear, it took real effort to put their hand back onto the steering wheel. It turned out to be the last F1 race using the banked track.

Next day, after many negotiations, we gathered again at the two garages and were finally allowed to examine the remains of the car. The Ferrari Chief Engineer, Carlo Chiti – who was an imposing figure – and their Racing Manager, Romolo Tavoni, were also present. Chiti examined both cars and indicated to us that in his opinion their engine in our chassis would beat the world!

The Italian officials then allowed us to remove the engine and leave Italy – which we did very rapidly. While all this was going on another car had been taken over to Austria by Bob Pearman and another mechanic. They had to drive the van and trailer non-stop to make it on time. A magnificent feat.

I was back in 1962 working on Jimmy's car, but unfortunately he had to retire with gearbox problems. This may have been the year I shared a room with Cedric (Selzer) on the second floor of a small hotel. At breakfast Cedric asked if I was aware that I talked in my sleep. Apparently, I said there was a cow on the balcony. He was so convinced that he got up to take a look!

Many years later, while on a trip to Monaco, Shirley and I drove to Monza in our small hire car and were asked at the gate if we were there to drive around the circuit on their open day – I don't think our insurance would have covered that. We did go in and looked at the old pits and paddock, then watched a few boy racers in their expensive cars doing a few laps with some not always reappearing. I had intended to look at what remained of the banking but it started to snow and we had a long journey back to Nice.

ENNA-PERGUSA

The latter derives from the Pergusa lake, which encircles the track, and the former due to its location near to the Sicilian city of the same name. It never held a Grand Prix, but we raced there on many occasions in non-championship events.

In 1963, Cedric and myself had to fly out to Switzerland to collect two cars that had been left at the airport by our colleagues Dick Scammell and Ted Woodley, after the cars had competed in the non-championship race in Sweden at Karlskoga. Our job was to take them by road to the ferry at Naples and on to Sicily. As the aircraft descended we could see our Ford transporter and trailer in the car park with flat tyres, so not a good start to our epic journey!

The transporter was a lengthened flat-back Ford 400E Thames (the famous PMT), with a modified Ford Zephyr engine and a 6-speed gearbox. There was just enough room in the cab for two people and their luggage. A car sat on a platform behind the cab and underneath were lockers containing fuel, tools, spares etc... The second car was towed behind on a trailer. It was painted in British Racing Green with the Team Lotus logo on the sides. We could travel at up to 90mph but it had a habit of puncturing tyres, due to them being unable to be used at that speed. We would carry ten spare wheels/tyres, so we could complete most of the journeys undertaken.

We put our luggage and tools into PMT, changed the wheels and set off for sunny Sicily. The intention was to go via the railway tunnel under the Alps to save some precious time, but we arrived too late, so had to take the route over the Alps at night. As we began to climb up the mountain pass PMT started to boil so we had to stop several times to let the engine cool down. This was getting serious as we had to catch the ferry from Naples to Palermo, and we couldn't afford to miss the sailing.

With our water supply almost exhausted, cascading water was heard. We stopped in the hope it was accessible to us and discovered it was a mountain waterfall, so in complete darkness we emptied oil from a can and tied string to it, before lowering it in the hope of collecting some much needed water. Much to our relief we were successful. We struggled up the mountain to a small restaurant, where after eating we were given a huge glass carboy of water which we strapped on the back of PMT and continued our journey through the night, topping up the radiator regularly.

Arriving at the Swiss/Italian border the customs officers refused to let us enter as we didn't have our carnets (paperwork) correctly stamped from the Sweden to Switzerland journey. We pleaded with them for several hours, offering them photographs, stickers and wheel badges etc... in an effort to let us proceed. With time slipping away and the real possibility of missing the ferry, we had a stroke of luck when one of the officers came over to us making a forearm 'gesture' while saying "Profumo" and "Christine Keeler"! We all had a good laugh, then he opened the barrier for us – what was a big scandal at the time turned into good news for us.

With many miles still to go, but now on flat ground, we pushed PMT on with no overheating problems. On the way we also had to call in at Valerio Colotti's factory to collect gearbox spares. After a few glasses of wine we continued on our way to Naples, encountering yet another problem when the propshaft fell off! We spent some time fixing this as best as we could and then very slowly continued to the port.

Arriving at the dockside we saw the ship about to slip her moorings and sail off. Again, we bribed, pleaded and almost begged on our knees for them to let us board as Chapman would not have been too happy if we didn't make it. The officer in charge of loading must have felt sorry for the two bleary-eyed, bedraggled mechanics standing in front of him and agreed to lower the ramp and let us onboard. It was an overnight trip so we finally had a chance to recuperate and rest for a while.

Finally, upon reaching Palermo we saw the smiling face of Andrew Ferguson, whom after we had contacted him earlier about the journey from Palermo to Enna had flown out to Sicily to help us as it would have been impossible to drive over the mountains with PMT's current problems. Andrew was the Team Manager and had a very fraught job under Colin Chapman, which he handled brilliantly, always managing to sort out our problems.

He had organised alternative transport for PMT's cargo and us in the form of a huge tipper truck, which I think was normally used for carrying sand, so very old and tatty. Alongside Andrew was Luigi, the small but muscular driver of this 'outfit'. With the aid of several dockers, passengers and some wooden planks we managed to get the two cars plus gear lifted up manually onto his truck. Also, Andrew had borrowed a large white open Cadillac from the Dutch racing driver, Count Carel Godin de Beaufort, so in convoy we set off for Enna while PMT was taken away for repair.

Sicily did not appear to have more than 100 yards of straight road on the island and was full of mountains. We arrived in Enna to another problem – unloading the truck. This was solved by reversing up to the many steps of a church, and with the aid of some friendly locals plus two long wooden planks we eased the cars off and down the steps. Quite a sight for the local congregation!

Using the Cadillac we towed the cars to the circuit where we prepared them for practice, before going back to our unfinished, three-quarter built hotel that had concrete spiral steps inside with no handrail or sides.

The circuit was surrounded by mountains, with a very smelly lake in the middle – complete with snakes – which lapped up just behind our pit area, which consisted of a few corrugated iron bays. The pit lane was narrow but did have an Armco safety barrier – well, sort of. On the

I'm alongside Trevor while he gets ready for the start.

opposite side of the track were lumps of loose rock with a rock face behind – no Armco barriers there – that had been hewed out to form the circuit.

Trevor Taylor was driving Jim's car as Jim was not prepared to race in Italy until the von Trips accident had been cleared up, as he could have been detained as mentioned in the Monza memories. Peter Arundell was in the number two car. Trevor commented that Jim's steering wheel was lower onto his knees than his own and was concerned that he would not be able to get out quickly in an emergency. There was nothing we could do at this point so it stayed as it was.

The race was under way with Trevor dicing wheel-to-wheel with the Ferrari of arch-rival Lorenzo Bandini until the Italian's car touched one of the loose rocks that shot up from his rear wheel, hitting Trevor on the head. This caused him to lose control and he crashed into the Armco barrier, tearing off the gearbox and part of the rear suspension. The remaining parts of the car flew upside down and deposited Trevor onto the centre of the track (no seatbelts in those days), before landing on the rocks and catching fire. He sat up in the middle of the track absolutely stunned by the event and we ran and picked him up, carrying him to the ambulance. The race was still continuing during all this and the ambulance couldn't get across the circuit to the hospital until it had finished. I sat with Trevor, who was shaken and bruised, but more concerned that he had scraped his watch on the track and torn his overalls! We watched the rest of the race through the ambulance window, while the driver gave us bottles of Coke after taking the tops off with his teeth. We then saw Arundell having a close race with Bandini and we thought Oh no not again! But he managed to stay in the race and finish second.

When the flag finally dropped the ambulance, with myself and an unhappy Trevor, headed off very fast and quite dangerously to a distant hospital, where he had a check-up and was given the all clear. If he had been wearing a seatbelt in his car it would have been a different story, as he would probably have been killed. The back end and gearbox, along with some of the rear suspension of the stricken car, had flown over the Armco barrier in the accident and skidded down the pit lane at high speed towards the last of the bays, which was used by Ferrari. As the mechanics were signalling their drivers close to the barrier they saw the Lotus parts hurtling down towards them. They pushed their team back and, unfortunately, some of them ended up in the not so sweet lake. Later we were to recover most of the damaged parts.

In the evening there was a prize giving ceremony at a floodlit old castle. After the prizes were given out and the usual boring speeches were made by the Auto Club and Town Mayor etc... the drivers were invited to an arena in the castle yard to fight small bulls, which we all found great fun.

The next day the truck was loaded with everything, ready to head for Palermo – but we had to wait for the start/finish money to be paid out so we had a drive around the town in Carel's Cadillac. While chatting to some local girls we were informed by their mother – whilst drawing a line across her throat – that Guilamo (Mafia boss) would sort us out. At this point we decided it would be prudent to collect the money and make a hasty exit towards Palermo. The day had been hot, and as we drove around the mountains in the evening we stopped off for a Coke and sat on a bank. In the now pitch black we heard a groaning, puffing noise. With a large amount of race money still on us and the thought of the Mafia still in our minds we jumped back into the car, driving off at speed – only to see an old Sicilian riding on a donkey!

Back in Palermo, PMT still wasn't ready so we had two days to explore the town and lay on the beach. Eventually all was ready and, before setting off, Andrew said if we drove all night we could have an evening out in Cannes, which we jumped at. While driving through France towards Calais we suffered more punctures, so stopped in a town to take several wheels and tyres to the local garage for repair. A gendarme pointed out that we were illegally parked, to which Andrew said, "Don't take any notice, he will go away" – which he did, only to swiftly return with a police van. We were then arrested and taken to the local police station. After a strong lecture we were fined the equivalent amount of £50. Definitely not motorsport enthusiasts!

Every time we stopped in Italy or France people would gather round, excited to see the cars – especially Trevor's wreck! Arriving back in good old Blighty people would walk by and say, "Trust no one was hurt old boy!" This turned out to be an expensive trip for Team Lotus.

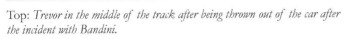

Top: *Trevor in the middle of the track after being thrown out of the car after the incident with Bandini.*

Above: *Trevor being rescued.*

Right: *I help carry the shaken Trevor away for medical attention.*

All photos © Contino Enna (Italian newspaper).

With Graham Hill, Colin Chapman and Tony Rudlin, the Team Manager of the Herts and Essex Aero Team.

Jackie Oliver's type 48 in the assembly area.

MONTJUICH PARK (BARCELONA)

My only visit was for the Formula Two race in 1968, which turned out to be a poignant time in my career.

The previous year – now working at Lotus Components/Developments – I was mechanic to Jackie Oliver, when he was racing the type 41 in Formula Three. Jackie asked me if I would be interested in running him in F2 in 1968 under the Herts and Essex Aero Club umbrella. The club was owned by an ex-Speedway rider, Roger Frogley, who I agreed to meet to discuss terms. The plan was to run a Type 48 in conjunction with the works cars of Jimmy and Graham (Hill). They would run in Gold Leaf colours, while we would keep the green and yellow original team colours.

After a satisfactory meeting at Hethel, he asked me to refuel his private plane. Along with Brian 'The Broom'

Leighton, churns of fuel and a short length of rubber hose attached to a funnel, I began to refuel the plane. Once filled up I pulled out the funnel, only to discover that it was minus the rubber hose! I spent a while fishing around with welding wire and long nose pliers to remove said object, but to no avail. Acutely embarrassed, I had to explain to my new boss what had happened. Fortunately, he took it in good part and just ordered another plane from the Aero Club to collect him and Jackie. An aircraft technician arrived the next day to strip out the fuel tank – what a start to a new venture.

Barcelona was the first F2 race of the season and we didn't have a transporter, so the Team Manager, Tony Rudlin, turned up with a Ford Zephyr and trailer. The three of us (Tony, Jackie and I), toolbox and equipment squeezed into the Zephyr with the 48 on a trailer and headed for the ferry. At about 75mph the trailer started to snake badly and to my surprise Jackie accelerated up to 90mph to stabilize the outfit! Most frightening, but it worked.

The temporary circuit was a real test, using roads running through the magnificent Montjuich Park. As was the norm with street circuits it was lined with Armco barriers, which left no margin for error.

Race day was sunny and the cars had to be pushed onto the grid, while the drivers were asked to walk beside them without wearing their helmets so the crowds could identify them – which I thought was a good idea. Jackie ran well in the race to finish fifth behind Jackie Stewart, Henri Pescarolo, Chris Amon and Piers Courage, so he was in good company. Jimmy's race ended on the first lap when he was hit from behind by Jacky Ickx, while Graham Hill in the other works car also retired due to over-revving his engine at around half distance. Their retirements meant they could both grab an early flight back to England. It was the last time I saw Jimmy.

While the works team headed for the next race at Hockenheim a week later, we headed back to England due to Jackie having a commitment to drive a Lotus 47 in the BOAC 6-hour race at Brands Hatch.

The cars of Jimmy and Innes in the paddock.

ZELTWEG

It was a military airfield based in a valley surrounded by mountains. The layout was marked out with straw bales – even the pit area – which made things extremely dangerous for all of us. With no pits or paddock, all the teams worked on their respective cars in an enormous hangar. The perimeter runway area used as part of the circuit was very bumpy, causing many cars to retire with suspension and driveshaft failures.

In 1961, when we raced there it was a non-championship race – not uncommon in that era – given the title of the Flugplatzrennen. Innes Ireland won from pole position in the Lotus 21-Climax, while Jim Clark finished fourth in a similar car. Innes also took fastest lap. On days like this he was brilliant, but on others...

After the race we all went back to our hotel to celebrate Innes' victory, most of the drivers with their wives or girlfriends: Jimmy, Trevor (Taylor), Graham and Bette (Hill), Bruce and Pat (McLaren), Tony and Gail (Maggs), Tim and Jenny (Parnell), and of course Innes, along with many others.

During the evening two Scottish lads came in wearing their tartan kilts and started to chat with Jimmy and Innes. After a while they all disappeared, and when Jimmy and

Innes returned they were wearing the lads' kilts. They both proceeded to give a rendition of the Highland Fling! Innes went and sat on Bette Hill's lap before dancing around and lifting up his kilt, which gave Trevor Taylor the opportunity to grab a nearby cactus plant and pop it up somewhere sensitive. Innes was picking out cactus needles for days afterwards.

Nearly all the drivers and mechanics would stay in the same hotel and we all knew each other on first name terms, and shared a good camaraderie. One evening I went along with Cedric to join some of the BRM guys: Dennis 'Sheriff' Perkins, Alan Challis, Cyril Atkins (Chief Mechanic) and Len (their truck driver) for a night out. Compared to us at Team Lotus – who had our old transporter and hired cars to run about in – the BRM team not only had a transporter, but also a Raymond Mays converted Ford Zephyr estate car for the mechanics. After a good evening out we all piled into the Zephyr for the return journey. On the way back we all urged Len, who was normally a steady driver, to 'give it some wellie'. This was great until we took a humpback bridge at around 90mph, which left us all intact but with very sore heads.

Our hotel was a large, very old coaching inn. The main entrance hall had a very high roof with wooden beams across it. One night Cedric and I came back from sampling the local hostelry, much the worse for wear after an excess of the excellent local brew, and decided to remove one of the posters advertising the race and pin it on the highest beam – a matter of about 20ft up. This was successfully achieved by using the dining tables and chairs. On the way back to our rooms we noticed the other residents had left their shoes out for cleaning. These were removed to the hall and left in a great pile.

Cedric made it to practice the next morning, but I remained in my room with a pounding head and a big hangover. Later I thumbed a lift to the circuit and had to endure the noise of racing cars and a rollicking from a rather angry Chief Mechanic, Jim Endruweit. It was lesson learned – well at least until the next time.

In 1964, the track surface was even worse than before and it would end up being the last time it was used for Formula One cars. Both our cars broke driveshafts due to the bumpy track and many other cars suffered handling problems due to the surface. One such was Phil Hill (Cooper), who spun into the straw bales and then the car caught fire. Phil tried to put the fire out but was restrained by race officials, while the car was completely burnt out. Lorenzo Bandini won the race – what turned out, sadly, to be his only Grand Prix victory.

Jo Bonnier with Rob Walker Racing mechanic Tony Cleverly.

Left to right: Dennis 'Sheriff' Perkins (BRM mechanic), Bette Hill, Tony Rudd (BRM), unknown lady, Graham Hill, Jim Clark, Wally Hassan (Coventry Climax), only just visible, Jenny Parnell, Tim's wife.

Mike Hailwood posing for the camera. These photos show the flat, featureless nature of the circuit.

Mike Spence and mechanic Bill Cowe at the 1964 race. Note the straw bales that defined the track layout.

SPA-FRANCORCHAMPS

This was a long (over eight miles), very fast road circuit situated in the Ardennes forest. It had sweeping bends down the side of a valley, near to the village of Stavelot, then climbed back up the other side. With ditches and pine trees either side and no barriers it proved the ability of the best drivers.

The pits and start line were on a downhill section, which meant that it was necessary for the mechanics to put wedges of folded up 'tank tape' under the rear tyres to stop the car rolling down the hill when the driver was holding the car on the clutch ready for the flag to drop. As the cars accelerated away all these pieces of tape were flung up in the air. Ferrari were rather unwisely using metal wedges, which had to be retrieved when the grid had moved off.

It was here that one of our mechanics, Dick Scammell, was dangerously caught out standing on the grid when the cars moved off. Jimmy had a problem and Dick rushed over to the car to give assistance – then the starting flag was dropped. He stood frozen in front of the Lotus as the cars fled by, then Jimmy drove off to follow the pack. Dick was lucky not to have been killed.

We prepared our cars in a local garage owned by George Lecoq in Stavelot, a picturesque Belgian village with houses around a central square, a fountain and surrounded by forest covered hills. This was an ideal setting for us mechanics as we could drive the cars up to the pits on four miles of the road circuit, something we all enjoyed doing. Later, after practice, we would drive them back down the other half of the circuit.

Cedric and I would drive the cars back to the garage as fast as we dared. Driving down the valley the vibrations in the car gave us double vision. Amazed at this we asked the drivers about it. Needless to say, they said it was normal and they just got used to it.

One night we worked until about 1am, then had to walk back to our hotel across the main square of this pretty village. It occurred to us that, as we were still awake, why not the Belgians? So once again a small bomb was made, and set off in the middle of the square, resulting in lights coming on in most of the village and also the surrounding hills.

Trevor (Taylor) had a big accident in practice on a fast curve at the bottom end of the circuit when a bolt broke and sent him off at 120mph over the grass, across a ditch and into a hut used for storing road maintenance equipment. Fortunately for Trevor it was a wooden hut and the impact sent him back onto the circuit. He was badly bruised and shaken up, but otherwise looked okay, so we quickly prepared the test car for him to start the race in on the following day. We thought he would probably only manage a few laps.

On race day Trevor was very stiff and in great pain but he decided to start (this was important as the team then received start money). We gently lowered him into the car and sent him off for his warm-up lap. He managed a few laps before retiring to the pits (officially with low oil pressure problems), a very brave effort on his behalf.

When we examined the shunted car we found that the only parts of the car holding the front end to the back end were the rubber fuel tanks, thus making him one lucky driver.

It was quite common for the track conditions to be vastly different from one end to the other, due to the circuit's length and part of it being at the bottom of the valley which was often wet in the undulating forest area. This could cause many a hairy moment for the drivers, as was the case with Jackie Stewart, who was trapped in his car by the steering wheel after an accident. Graham Hill stopped and gave him assistance to get out. From then on, Jackie had a spanner taped to the steering wheel!

Jimmy was very quick at Spa and won the Grand Prix

four years running (1962-65). One year, when he came past the pits on his first lap in heavy rain, we thought there had been an accident as no other cars could be heard or seen. We then realised that he was a brilliant ten seconds ahead of the pack.

In 1960 another Lotus driver, Mike Taylor (no relation to Trevor), went missing in practice and couldn't be found anywhere on the track. His mechanics asked all the drivers that came into the pits if they had seen him, but to no avail. The practice session was stopped while race officials began to search for him. He was eventually found some distance from the circuit having crashed through the forest, ending up at the bottom of a hill. His steering column was broken and he was severely injured. They managed to get him out of the car and he was taken to hospital with severe injuries, from which he eventually recovered. This all happened shortly after Stirling Moss's serious accident, when a wheel flew off. Luckily he also survived, although with serious injuries.

We arrived at Spa early one year and with time on our hands decided to do a couple of laps in the team's hire car. As we passed the pits we noticed many splendid flags up high on flagpoles. One had a large wire wheel on it, with the description of a Belgian Auto Club. We all thought how good it would look in our workshop back at Cheshunt. We parked the car in the paddock and sent our fittest mechanic, Nick Garbett, up the pole to remove the flag on our behalf. As he was busy untying it the local police pulled up in the pit lane and proceeded to take their 'fag break'. While they were leaning against the bonnet of their car poor old Nick was hanging on for grim death. After ten minutes they drove off and Nick plummeted down, complete with flag. It took pride of position on our wall – a hard earned memento! Sadly, a few months later, Nick and his wife – who were newly married – lost their lives in a speedboat accident.

ZOLDER

I returned to Belgium in 1968, this time to the Zolder circuit with the Herts and Essex Aero Club Lotus 48. Surprisingly, we arrived a day early, which was very unusual as we were usually rushed off our feet preparing the car.

After parking the transporter, we sat in the Pits Hotel on a verandah overlooking the circuit on what was a nice sunny day. There were a few local racers doing some testing, one of whom was in an E-Type Jaguar, and another in a Super Vee single-seater. Jackie Oliver arrived with his girlfriend, Lynne, and we started to have a few beers. As the afternoon went on the Super Vee began to slowly catch up with the E-Type until eventually it was right on its tail. We thought the combination of the E-Type's top speed and the Vee's cornering power would make for some interesting viewing. The next time around neither appeared. A little while later a breakdown truck passed by with a very bent Jaguar on board. It reminded me of the early days at Snetterton when they held 'anything goes' practice sessions. This would include F1 cars, saloons, motorcycles and even sidecars. It wasn't good for the latter, especially on tight corners, when the passenger would lean out – often into the path of other vehicles. Exciting for the spectators but very dangerous. These sessions soon ceased and 20-minute separate sessions were introduced for cars of different formulae and bikes.

Back on the verandah it was time for our meal, so we ate in the hotel restaurant. It was a lavish affair and those who were seafood lovers could go to a huge aquarium and select their meal by pointing out the fish or lobster of their choice. These were then plucked out with a net and cooked (poor things!).

MONACO

This is the most glamorous of all the Grand Prix circuits, attracting a real who's who of not just the motor racing fraternity but also A-list celebrities, who all combine with the royal presence of Prince Rainier (and Princess Grace in those days) to give it a unique style and ambience. During my time it was the only circuit where the winner received his trophy and garland alone. No podium in the usual way, but a meeting with the Royal Highnesses on the stairs of the Royal Box was unique to Monaco. The presenting of garlands is long gone. The sponsors complained they covered up their logos on the driver's overalls.

> *The pits were simply a roadside area with our tools plus equipment kept in the small garden between the two roads. Working on cars was hairy, to say the least, as we had to keep an eye out for passing cars as well as remembering to keep our feet in!*

From a mechanic's point of view, it was less than glamorous and a really challenging environment to work in. The pits were simply a roadside area with our tools plus equipment kept in the small garden between the two roads. Working on cars was hairy, to say the least, as we had to keep an eye out for passing cars as well as remembering to keep our feet in!

While it was challenging, it did have its perks. The Tip Top bar was where all the teams congregated when possible, as working on the cars was often a day and night business. One year we were having a quiet(!) drink when things began to get rather boisterous and a group of young lads, worse the wear for alcohol, started throwing glasses out onto the road. This brought out the French riot police, who were not to be messed with – their policy was to walk in a line across the road and anyone in their way would be in trouble. The aforementioned four or five young lads danced in front of them and gave them rude signs. They were subsequently banged on the head with truncheons and disappeared through the line of police.

One night before practice the following day, Jimmy and Trevor took Dick, Cedric and myself for an unforgettable tour around the circuit in their hire car. Jimmy was driving and giving us a terrific ride when Trevor put his foot down over Jimmy's on the throttle pedal and we two-wheeled it round the next corner. Jimmy was terrified and so were we!

We stayed in a hotel at Eze Sur Mere, about six kilometres from Monaco, on the winding coast road. It was positioned just up a small hill behind the garage in which we prepared the cars. Our break from working was to have dinner seated in a small restaurant by the roadside on the bend near the garage, often watching the F1 drivers going into Monaco for the evening and giving it a 'boot full' past our tables! On one memorable evening while sitting outside the La Bananerie restaurant, 'Taffy' von Trips in his Ferrari came by in a four-wheel drift and we all stood up and applauded, much to his delight – so he turned around and repeated the manoeuvre. We called him Taffy because his full name was Wolfgang Alexander Albert Eduard Maximilian Reichsgraf Berghe von Trips. Far too long to fit on a pit board!

We were given a plentiful supply of red wine during our stay, both at the hotel and garage. This encouraged us to entice some of the new mechanics into a drinking competition, which resulted in them crawling on all fours up the hill to their beds.

Just down the road from our hotel was where Alf Francis, Tony Cleverly and another mechanic were staying. One evening while we were walking past we found Tony

Working on the cars in the garage at Eze Sur Mere in 1962. In the background are Peter Arundell and his wife Ricky (yellow dress).

Same location the following year. By the looks on our faces and the state of the cars, we have a few problems to sort.

Trevor Taylor lines up seventeenth on the grid for the 1962 race.
Jo Bonnier is alongside in a Porsche (2). The row ahead is the
BRM of Richie Ginther (8), and the Lola of Roy Salvadori.

Colin and Hazel Chapman sat on the team's toolboxes to do the timing and
lap charts at the 1963 race, while Dick Scammell alters the signalling board.

and the other mechanic (who was with Alf working on Stirling's Lotus of the Rob Walker Team) crawling past their hotel. At first sight we thought they were 'worse for wear' due to alcohol, but they just wanted to go to bed without passing the bar where Alf was installed for the rest of the evening.

The mention of Stirling brings back an amusing incident. During one wet practice he stopped by our pit area and stepped out of his car complaining of hot water on his feet caused by a leaking radiator. Cedric and I were busy working on Jimmy's car in the pouring rain, so Cedric was wearing a pair of clear plastic waterproof overalls. Typical of Stirling he made the comment that Cedric looked like a walking 'French letter'!

As mechanics we were very lucky as we had the pleasure of driving the cars from the garage to Monaco along the twisting coast road and through the tunnels, while the motor cycling gendarmes waved us on to go faster. This drive was a tremendous thrill for us, especially as Chapman and the other mechanics were sideways trying to keep up in their VW Beetle hire car, while the Bedford transporter followed on. The noise through the tunnels from the exhausts was magic. The Formula Three cars would practice very early in the morning and would roar past our garage at 7am. It was usually a good race even before reaching Monaco.

> *As mechanics we were very lucky as we had the pleasure of driving the cars from the garage to Monaco along the twisting coast road and through the tunnels, while the motor cycling gendarmes waved us on to go faster.*

The entry limit for the F1 cars was 16. Ten were invited – two cars each for works teams plus past winners, while the remaining places had to be fought for by practice times. There were usually over 20 cars practising. Some of the competitors even cut the front off the noses of their cars to increase the air flow into the radiator and to shorten the car for easier manoeuvring in circuit traffic.

Chapman decided to have super lightweight brackets to hold the rear roll bar onto the car. Jimmy was going well but the brackets broke and the bar was trailing along the ground behind him. The organisers insisted that we bring the car into the pits to remove the bar, so I went to the hairpin and stood on the garden wall, and as Jimmy came round I pointed to the pits. He didn't come in so we had to give him an 'IN' signal on the board as he came by the harbourside. When he finally stopped the offending bar

A cutting from an Italian newspaper showing me giving Jimmy the IN signal. Behind me with the cine camera is Jimmy's farming neighbour and friend Andrew Cowan. This photo also illustrates the 'garden' nature of the pit area.

had dropped off, so out he went again. The roll bar was never recovered – by us anyway! – probably ending up as the pride and joy of a spectator.

1961 saw a very tired Jack Brabham competing as he had just flown in from Indianapolis after qualifying at the Brickyard in his 2.7-litre Coventry Climax Cooper at 145.14mph. Innes Ireland had a monumental shunt when he became confused with the different gear shift gate on the ZF 5-speed gearbox that differed from the Colotti and selected second instead of fourth at about 100mph. Everything locked up whilst in the tunnel and he was very lucky to be thrown clear. He was taken to the Princess Grace Hospital where his leg was put into plaster.

We were joined in the pits by jazz musician Chris Barber, who owned a Lotus Elite that he sometimes raced. At the evening meal he played music on the wine jugs!

As Dan Gurney and Jimmy had to dash from Monaco to Indy, they went by speedboat around to Nice to catch their flight to America. After a very rough sea trip it was decided in future they would drive. This was a big problem as thousands of spectators were filling the roads on their way home.

Chapman had to be at Nice airport soon after the finish of the Grand Prix, so we all kept out of his way as no one wanted to go with him in the hire car. Unfortunately, he caught me and I had to be passenger in the VW Beetle. We fled away from Monaco on the wrong side of the road, cutting in when traffic approached head on, much to the annoyance of the French motorists who pointed at the hospital and held their fingers to their heads – most embarrassing for me. On the drive through Nice we nearly collided with an elderly woman crossing the road and soon had a motor cycling gendarme on our tail. Chapman said that when he pulled up at the airport he would run, and I was to follow with his briefcase! While the gendarme was putting his BMW onto its stand we ran into the airport building. When I crept out of the departure lounge the gendarme was waiting by the VW tapping his fingers on the roof. He asked the whereabouts of the driver and I pointed to the Boeing 707 just climbing into the blue sky. He let us off and I had a quiet drive back to the garage.

We all enjoyed racing at Monaco as the weather was usually very warm and the atmosphere very exciting. It was possible to hear some of the cars like the Matra go all around the circuit. This was music to our ears at the time, but now we all suffer with bad hearing – a price to pay. Ear defenders weren't available and you were considered a 'sissy' if you covered your ears with your hands.

A stroll around the harbour was mind blowing, with the enormous yachts and their crews constantly polishing and painting. Speedboats and wind surfers were in abundance, and on board there were dining tables complete with candelabras, set out on deck ready for dinner. Ferraris, Mercedes and Rolls Royces were parked on the harbour to complete the scene.

> "We all enjoyed racing at Monaco as the weather was usually very warm and the atmosphere very exciting. It was possible to hear some of the cars like the Matra go all around the circuit. This was music to our ears at the time, but now we all suffer with bad hearing – a price to pay."

Jimmy took the whole team to the Sporting Club of Monaco, where we were entertained by Johnny Hallyday, the then top rock star of France. The place was full of ageing millionaires with their young 'ladies' on their arms. This trip cost Jimmy a tremendous amount of money, but we were all very grateful and thoroughly enjoyed it. When we left the garage to return to England we left them 100 gallons of Esso fuel and, in return, they packed us up a feast of sandwiches, grapes and wine.

I have since returned to Eze Sur Mere and the garage is still there, but converted into a private house. Also, l have returned to Monaco, when we were staying in Nice. We rented a small car and travelled to the principality. We walked and drove around the circuit, now with the swimming pool built over part of the old layout. The circuit still goes past what was the pits, but the gasworks and hairpin have now gone. We had lunch near the Tabac corner and spoke to a shop owner, who invited us into a room behind his shop to see many photos of racing in the early days at Monaco that his father had taken. A hidden gem.

Clockwise from top left:

During some of the quieter moments – of which they weren't many – I would capture some of the other non-Lotus drivers. Bruce McLaren kindly poses for me.

The stylish Lorenzo Bandini does the same.

While Dan Gurney looks his usual, relaxed self.

Jimmy's car in the pits at Monaco in 1962. This image illustrates perfectly the safety standards of the time. No pit lane barriers, straw bales, single-tier Armco, and spectators close to the action.

" *The general consensus of opinion was that circuits like Monaco, Monza, the Nürburgring and Spa-Francorchamps were some of the most dangerous, due mainly to their high-speed, but also the lack of safety barriers meant that a mechanical/ tyre failure or driver error often resulted in going off the circuit into trees, with the outcome often proving fatal.* "

6

SAFETY ISSUES

In this chapter I would like to highlight some of the safety issues that were around in the sixties, and the improvements that have taken place partly due to the efforts of Sir Jackie Stewart and the Grand Prix Drivers' Association (GPDA). Drivers and spectator casualties were high, and it was time for change.

The general consensus of opinion was that circuits like Monaco, Monza, the Nürburgring and Spa-Francorchamps were some of the most dangerous, due mainly to their high-speed, but also the lack of safety barriers meant that a mechanical/tyre failure or driver error often resulted in going off the circuit into trees, with the outcome often proving fatal. It was on these circuits where the very talented drivers could easily find time over those less blessed.

It was widely accepted by us mechanics that it was a dangerous time to be involved, but we all knew the risks. Looking back, this was a very blasé approach, but then again we were all young and infallible!

If, during practice or a race your car didn't pass the pits it was not unusual for the mechanics to set off and walk along the edge of the circuit to find your car and diagnose what the problem might be. Looking back this was a very dangerous thing to do, but we treated it as the norm. Some of the drivers would even pull up or point out where to find your driver. We would then work on the car by the side of the track, or near to it, keeping very alert for any other car that may lose control and come towards you. It

was not unusual to sprint across the circuit during a race to attend to a driver or his car.

The pits at Zolder were lower than the circuit, and on one occasion Jochen Rindt was hit from behind at the start of a Formula Two race, with the front wheels of his Brabham ending up in our pit box. We all had to heave the car back onto the pit lane for him to continue.

The pits at Monte Carlo were just a narrow garden between the curved straight from Tabac corner to the Gasworks Hairpin and the straight leading to Ste Devote. With no pit wall or guard rail you were working on the car in the pit lane with your legs and feet stuck out almost onto the circuit itself. It goes without saying, this was a hazardous occupation.

Many of the circuits had no protection for the mechanics and team personnel who were in the pits. The cars would just turn off the circuit and come flying into the narrow pit lane at speed. I have witnessed many a collision, and even mechanics knocked down.

It wasn't just the pits that had no or little protection. The circuits would be lined with straw bales as crash barriers (useless for safety but handy for photographers, and as braking marker points), but no good in preventing a car from going into trees or even into spectators.

Things had to change, and thankfully for all concerned, numerous improvements were implemented. Some examples are: The very steep, concrete banking at Monza began to crumble, so became unsafe and was never used again; The Nürburgring had some Armco fitted and some trees felled, but due to its length (just over 14 miles) it was impossible to marshal properly, and following Niki Lauda's fiery accident in the 1976 German Grand Prix Formula One never returned. They did return in the eighties to a modern, shorter layout. The old circuit is still there and is used extensively for lower forms of racing, and for the public to sample in their road cars or motorbikes; The Spa circuit, which used public roads, was shortened from its original eight miles to approximately half of that by introducing a permanent section which removed the flat-out blast down to the Masta Kink and back through the forest and farm buildings to La Source. The start was on the downhill straight leading to Eau Rouge. This proved difficult for the drivers to hold the cars stationary on and necessitated pads under the rear wheels to stop them rolling. Eventually, the start was moved to the flat straight leading to La Source, and a new pit complex built alongside; Monaco moved the start/finish line from the harbour front just before the Gasworks Hairpin to in front of the Royal Box, thus making Ste Devote the first corner. A proper pit lane with guard rail protection was a welcome improvement. Some escape roads were introduced, a couple of run off areas, better lighting in the tunnel and cranes to lift cars off the circuit. All the above helped to improve the safety standards considerably.

Another major improvement was the starting procedure, which was somewhat haphazard and disorganised but involved some real characters, especially Toto Roche and Louis Chiron, who dropped the flag at Reims and Monaco, respectively. They would stand in front of the grid with the flag, then walk slowly to the side of the track before dropping it for the start. On some occasions they were missed by inches, having failed to make sure they were safely out of the way when the drivers dropped their clutches. In some ways it was a shame, as their antics kept us amused, and the drivers on their toes.

Year by year improvements were made, but while safer, it still remained far from safe, unlike the safety standards of today. The Grand Prix Medical Unit organised by Louis Stanley of BRM was a great idea in principle, but suffered from opposition from a few organisers, and it being the brainchild of 'Big Lou' didn't exactly endear it to people. The unit did play a part in the aftermath of Bandini's fatal accident at Monaco in 1967. Nowadays, doctors in high-performance vehicles follow the cars after the start, with helicopters standing by to attend to casualties within minutes.

The standard of the marshals has improved beyond all recognition. While they remain volunteers, they are now properly equipped with fireproof, luminous overalls and have undergone considerable safety training.

> *The standard of the marshals has improved beyond all recognition. While they remain volunteers, they are now properly equipped with fireproof, luminous overalls and have undergone considerable safety training.*

The cars themselves have also undergone considerable improvements, the main one being the introduction of the aluminium monocoque to replace the tubular, spaceframe construction, which could easily trap the driver when involved in an accident. Monocoques were much stronger and safer, particularly regarding how the fuel was carried. In a spaceframe chassis the fuel tanks were made of aluminium and shaped to fit between the chassis tubes. Consequently, these often leaked, and drivers ended up sitting in a pool of petrol. Flexible, foam filled aircraft-type fuel tanks were fitted inside the monocoque. This was much safer – the foam inside stopped surge and slowed leakage if the tank was punctured in an accident.

Aligned with the improved fuel tanks was the use

of plumbed-in fire extinguisher systems, as opposed to the small hand-held type clipped onto the chassis by the dashboard, which proved completely useless. Sometimes they would fall off and rattle around the car. On one occasion Innes Ireland threw his out of the car whilst passing the pits at 100mph, and it bounced all the way down the pit road. The plumbed-in system took some mastering, with several manufacturers trying new ideas with varying activating systems from manual, electrical, G-force and flame detection sensors. They all had their problems. The push button electrical systems could be accidentally fired off by the driver or mechanics with their spanners. The G-Force type could be activated by just a small shunt, and the flame detection sensors could be fired off with the colour of the bodywork as the McLaren team found out when fitting their 'day-glo' panels! All the extinguishers suffered the same problem regarding the contents. The chemicals used would quickly corrode the car, so it had to be cleaned off immediately. I'm happy to report that all of the above problems were overcome with the fitting of push buttons inside and outside of the cockpit, with the contents of the extinguisher piped directly into the cockpit and engine bay in the event of an accident.

Another area of car improvements was the introduction of cut off (master) switches inside the cockpit and also outside, enabling the driver or outside assistance to disconnect the electrical system. This was a good move, as were seat belts with six fixing points; two shoulder straps, two waist straps and two crotch straps, all with quick release buckles – a big step in safety, holding the drivers securely in their seats.

On the driver front, multi-layer flame proof overalls, balaclavas, underwear, socks and gloves were introduced, offering considerably more protection than the blue Swixtell overalls and waterproofs which they had used previously. Open face helmets with Spitfire Mk2 goggles – plus a spare pair worn round the neck – were replaced with full-face versions. Rain on visors or goggles caused a big problem and some drivers had a pad fixed to their gloves to sponge off the water. Graham Hill thought he had the answer by fixing a circular spinning clear disc to the front of his helmet which would fling off the water (as on Navy ships). This worked well until he moved his head and the gyroscopic effect nearly tore it off.

No matter what head protection was worn, the driver's head was always vulnerable in single-seaters due to the inadequate one-piece, bent steel roll-over hoops which were always lower than the driver's head, so of little use if the car overturned. These were replaced by braced roll-over hoops that had to be a regulated distance above the top of the driver's helmet, so if you had a tall driver you had to make a new hoop to meet the regulations. They also contained a headrest to prevent whiplash.

Colin (Chapman) introduced a double windscreen to allow water to be forced up and over the driver's helmet. This proved successful, but we lost about 150rpm compared to the conventional screen. The loss of revs wasn't that crucial in wet conditions.

Finally, tyre technology was revolutionised by the introduction of slick tyres. The cornering speeds increased, but overall the racing was safer. In the sixties, Dunlop were the only manufacturers of racing car tyres. In Formula One we used the narrow, treaded R5. There were two versions, distinguished by a green spot for the dry and a yellow spot for the wet. Colin suggested that the softer compound wet tyres would give improved grip and would last the distance in a dry race. To try and stay in front of the other teams we repainted over the yellow spots with green paint, and the ruse worked well, but in the end became very confusing!

We always thought that the tyre fitters had an easier job than us, as after practice was over they could pack up and return to their hotels, while we stayed and worked well into the night and more often than not, all night.

A Lotus 30 mock-up ready for display at the Racing Car Show. It was basically a body and wheels.

The type 30 outside the factory at Cheshunt waiting to be loaded up.

"*I made the decision to leave Team Lotus at the end of the 1964 season – mainly to spend more time at home – and was offered a position with Lotus Developments (later to become Lotus Components, then Lotus Racing).*"

7

LOTUS DEVELOPMENTS

I made the decision to leave Team Lotus at the end of the 1964 season – mainly to spend more time at home – and was offered a position with Lotus Developments (later to become Lotus Components, then Lotus Racing). They were based at Cheshunt, so it was just a matter of moving departments.

We worked on several prototype racing cars, including the Lotus 30 with Ford 4727cc engine modified by the Lotus engine development department. This was not a particularly good model and proved difficult for the drivers due to many problems. The car had a backbone chassis with a centre fuel tank and aluminium fuel tanks down either side of the bodywork, which was wrapped in foam sheeting and covered by a fibreglass panel pop riveted in – very crude!

When we finished building the production cars in the upper workshop (above the components stores) they were lowered down to the ground via a gantry and hoist. I was unsure how to attach the car safely to the hoist and asked Colin Chapman what he thought was the best way. He told me to hook the hoist onto the rollover hoop. To my mind, this didn't look strong enough to take the weight due to it being secured with some small bolts, but he was right. I completed the task regularly with no problems.

Ian Walker Racing had the first car for Jim Clark to drive and he came second at Aintree. Several cars were built and then, with many updates, they became the Lotus 40 (same as the 30 but with ten more problems!). A

The type 40 at Silverstone in 1966 ready to be evaluated by Jack Sears.

Jack behind the wheel.

Two Team type 40s with the customer car destined for A.J. Foyt nearest the camera.

The great Juan Manuel Fangio was in the area, so dropped in for a look.

5.3-litre engine was built but blew up. The McLarens and Lolas were far better sports cars at the time. 'Gentleman' Jack Sears tested three of the Lotus 40 cars at Silverstone in early 1966, as he had already raced a type 30. These were two Team cars and one for a customer, a certain A.J. Foyt from America. Jack unfortunately damaged his wrist in an accident whilst testing.

In one race (I believe it was Goodwood) Jim Clark came into the pits with rear suspension problems, so the back was jacked up to sort it out. Colin ordered it to be refuelled at the same time, which was duly done and the car sent out again to race. It was then that Colin realised that the fuel had been put in whilst still on the jack and at an angle, so not enough had gone in. He was so angry that he chased one of the poor mechanics down the pit lane, but the car only completed a few more laps before retiring.

A Lotus 41 outside the Hethel factory flanked by numerous Europa bodyshells.

Between 1964 and 1965 we sold 33 of these cars, some of which were supplied in kit form.

During 1965 we built the prototype Lotus 41 F3 car which was tested and raced by Jackie Oliver. I used to take the car from Cheshunt up to Snetterton for testing and, as I was on my own, I would do a few laps to warm the car up before Jackie arrived to put it through its paces. On one occasion I was preparing the car at the factory and I noticed that one of the magnesium wheel spokes had a blowhole right through it, so I changed it and set off for Snetterton. On my return I was told that Fred Bushell – who was one of the Lotus directors – wanted to see me. I was slightly concerned as to why he wanted to see me, and when I entered his office he said, "I am going to give you a right rollicking!" Almost immediately he laughed and said, "Only joking!" He went on to say that I had saved the 41 project by noticing the faulty wheel, which had been missed by the inspection department and the tyre fitting shop. He then slipped a £10 note in my hand – a large

amount in those days. I left the office very relieved and extremely happy.

Later works supported 41s were run by Charles Lucas Racing for Piers Courage and American Roy Pike as drivers. Lotus Components then went on to build the Type 41 F2 car in 1967 for Jackie Oliver, and then the Type 41X for John Miles. Both would graduate to the F1 team; Jackie in 1968 following Jim Clark's tragic demise and John the following year, principally to develop the four-wheel-drive type 63.

I was asked to drive over to Modena in Italy to the Novamotor engine development shop to collect two modified Lotus twin-cam engines. Accompanying me, and taking turns to drive the company Bedford van, was Peter Arundell, who after showing great promise as Formula One team-mate to Jimmy in the early races of the 1964 season, was unfortunately involved in a high-speed accident at Reims. The resulting injuries kept him out of the cockpit in 1965. He made his comeback in January

1966 in a non-championship F1 race in South Africa, but he was never quite the same. It was a cold winter's day when we took the cross-channel ferry to Belgium and booked into a small hotel. Early next morning, just before we were about to depart, we found the van's engine was frozen solid. On thawing it out we found the cylinder head was cracked, so we were unable to continue. We managed to make contact with Cheshunt and were told to leave the van – they sent out a van and trailer to collect the stricken Bedford – and to hire a car (which turned out to be a VW Beetle) to continue our journey.

We drove down through France and over the snow-covered Alps to Modena, only to find the engines were not ready! After two days of waiting Peter had to fly back to the UK, while I remained, getting very frustrated as the engineers took long siestas and worked slowly. Eventually, after the engines had been run up on the dynamometer, I loaded them onto the backseat of the Beetle causing the car to sink down on its suspension. I set off to return over the Alps in heavy snow, which was an anxious time now that I was on my own. Lotus sent a van to the docks in Belgium to collect the engines, after which I returned the Beetle to the rental company with the ride height still on the low side! I parked it facing the office, and quickly made my escape.

I believe Lotus was the first company to construct a simulator. It consisted of a mock up Lotus single-seater with a large screen in front, then a three-foot clear plastic sphere cut in half with a flat top and a circuit mapped out with a lamp above it. Controls from the steering were attached to the sphere. As the steering wheel was turned it also moved the sphere showing a shadow of the circuit. It was a strange feeling to stand beside the driver and watch the movements and it could make you feel quite queasy. I had a go in it and suddenly came upon a double decker bus on the circuit. It was a model put there by Peter Warr! The whole thing was taken to garages and venues for the public

to have a go, but it was difficult to set up. I have described this to the best of my memory, having never seen it mentioned elsewhere.

In 1966, we outgrew the Cheshunt factory, and with the aid of Government grants, Colin decided to relocate to Norfolk and purchased the old Hethel airfield, which previously had been used by the United States Air Force 389th Bombardment Group, flying B-24 Liberators commanded by Hollywood star James Stewart during World War Two. It was the ideal location, with the runway used for testing and enabling Colin and visitors to land their aeroplanes. A few years later a complete test track was constructed. The building of a brand-new factory completed the impressive set-up.

Colin offered to pay all the moving expenses for as many of the workforce as he could who wished to relocate. Several of us decided to accept his offer as we wanted to stay. My first visit to the area and the half-built factory was in the winter, with snow and a biting wind blowing across the open runway. At this point I did question whether I had made the right decision to move from London, but I'm so glad I did.

In 1967, we arranged a reunion with our former colleagues who hadn't made the move. It was held at Wolseley Hall, Cheshunt, and in the car park was the Team Lotus type 11 (reg XAR11) with a 744cc Climax engine that was driven by Cliff Allison and Keith Hall to claim the 750cc class and the Index of Performance at Le Mans ten years earlier in 1957.

As a very keen water skier I soon discovered the beautiful Norfolk Broads and purchased a small aluminium speed boat with a 50hp Mercury outboard engine. Whenever possible I would rush home from work and get onto the water, skiing until darkness fell. David Lazenby, and development engineer, Roger Becker, also had speedboats. So, at the weekends we would all head off skiing, having made all types of equipment to use, from short trick skis to towing a round wooden disc (made at work!) on which we would place a chair to sit on and amuse holidaymakers.

On one occasion the owner of a large expensive cruiser, commonly known as a 'gin palace', asked us if it was possible to ski behind his boat. Although he had just filled up with fuel, making it quite heavy, Roger said he would give it a go. He successfully managed to slowly ski behind the enormous boat, but had to give up after a short while as the bow wave was about four feet high and this would upset fishermen on the banks and holidaymakers having tea on their hired boats. If caught by the Broads authorities we would have all been in serious trouble. Due to a change in the regulations water skiing is now restricted on the Broads to a very limited area.

Another interesting fact about Roger Becker is that he drove the 007 Lotus Esprit in one of the James Bond films after the stunt driver failed to turn up. He was there to maintain the car during filming.

Some years later (1971) Colin Chapman purchased Moonraker Boats and JCL Marine Ltd from John Berry. The first Moonraker was built in 1969 and was produced by Buxton Marine Services Ltd. The owner David Buxton also raced, so was known to Colin. Typical of Colin, he handled these huge high-powered cruisers with the same enthusiasm as he did his cars. Also, his innovative ideas turned the boat industry on its head.

There is an interesting book on the subject by Sarah O'Hara titled *Moonraker and JCL Marine Ltd: Colin Chapman's Boat Industry*.

In 1967, Formula Ford was born and the Lotus 51 was the first car to be built. Eventually, we went on to build over 200 cars. Basically, it was a modification of the Formula Junior Lotus 22 originally built in the early days at Cheshunt. The formula had initially used the 1.5-litre Cortina engine, but after a short time Ford preferred the 1600cc cross-flow unit, so this left many redundant new

1.5-litre engines in the workshop. This pleased us Cortina owners as we were able to purchase them for our cars. After finishing the prototype type 51 I tested it on the Hethel circuit. The car proved to be okay, but could not be driven too fast as the handling was poor due to the fact that we only had some odd springs to fit. I mentioned this to Components Manager, David Lazenby (ex-Team Lotus and Indy Chief Mechanic), before he decided to do a few laps himself. Several new Lotus Elans were parked in an area by the circuit, which was unfortunate for 'Laz' as he involuntarily chose this point to lose control and spin off the track, luckily going between the parked cars – but he wasn't so lucky when he went through a square sectioned wire fence. The wire caught him across his mouth and knocked his head back, luckily bending the small (roll hoop) head rest, saving further damage. If it had been a more substantial head rest he would have been decapitated. Colin was called and he rushed Laz to Norwich Hospital, covering his leather car seats in blood. After treatment Laz was left with permanent scars.

A Lotus 51 was made loosely road legal for Graham Arnold (Sales Director) with cycle wings, headlights and number plates. It was painted green and adorned with flower transfers. He drove this from Norfolk to the London Racing Car Show as a gimmick and was stopped several times en route by the police but not prosecuted. He also had a car sprayed brown with a dummy machine gun on the front, which he took to the nearby American Lakenheath base in the hope of selling them to the personnel who were keen Lotus customers.

It wasn't just single-seaters we were involved with. Between 1966 – 68 we built the type 47, which was derived from the Renault-engined Europa Type 46 production car. I returned to my race mechanic role with this car, with John Miles racing it several times. One of which was a victory in the GT race at Brands Hatch on Boxing Day, 1966 – turkey sandwiches for lunch!

The remains of the type 47 after the testing fire when John Miles was behind the wheel. © Nick Folliard.

The following year, at Oulton Park, we had gearbox problems in practice, which prevented John from completing a lap, resulting in him having to start at the back of the grid. For the race we had a set of new, unscrubbed slicks, so we decided to rough them up with surform files. Myself, Len Elston and two other mechanics sat on a wheel each and proceeded to file away. An American spectator stopped and asked what we were doing. The quick-witted Len replied, "Dunlop can't make them perfectly round so we are trimming them with this." To which the American replied, "Oh right." He walked off, leaving us falling off the wheels in fits of laughter!

John was always apprehensive before racing, so we guessed that when the flag dropped he would charge through the grid in destruct mode. He finished the race with deranged steering and several paint marks acquired from his climb up through the field. Complaints from more than one driver meant a visit to the race officials' office to be reprimanded for his over-spirited drive, but it did make a good race for the spectators.

On another occasion at Brands Hatch he had a lucky escape while testing the 47, when it caught fire. We heard him go past the back of the pits and into Surtees, when suddenly there was a spluttering and a whoosh sound. We ran towards it and saw John leaping out. Unfortunately, the cupboards alongside the circuit housing the fire extinguishers were locked up, so we were helpless and just had to watch the car burn out, leaving only the chassis and engine remaining. A phone call to an unhappy Colin Chapman was made and we returned home with the remains. The reason for the fire was never discovered at the time, but in a later engine fire that we managed to extinguish it was noticed that a seal in the Tecalemit-Jackson fuel injection system had burst and sprayed fuel directly onto the exhaust, so maybe that was the cause.

We built another 47 for the BOAC six-hour race at Brands Hatch, which had a large entry with works cars from Ferrari, Porsche and Chaparral. We were competing against mainly Porsches in the two-litre category. During scrutineering the officials wanted the steering put from lock to lock to check the wheel clearance from the body. We knew this was marginal, so we discreetly (we thought) lifted the back of the car slightly to compensate, but this was noticed and I was asked to step away from the car. We had to cut away the fibreglass wheel arches to give more clearance.

During practice we had a wheel fly off, which left us searching in the bushes for it before quickly returning to Hethel, where it was found that the angle on the central wing nut was incorrect – so the machine shop personnel had to be called in to work through the night making modifications.

All this meant that we had no time to practice our refuelling pit stops, so we just went through the process verbally as to who would open the vent cap, hold the funnel, fill the car from the fuel churn, wipe the screen and change the drivers' seats. Our driver pairing was John Miles and Jackie Oliver. The former was very tall, while the latter was quite short. This proved a problem when changing drivers as the whole seat had to be removed and changed to suit each of them.

Despite a few nudges here and there – all repaired with tank tape – and brake pads getting near their wear limit, we managed to win the two-litre class. The Porsches all suffered gearbox input shaft problems due to poor heat treatment in Germany. At post-race scrutineering we thought the car might be a bit on the light side, so as we pushed it along to the bay I slipped a piece of lead from up my sleeve into the exhaust pipe and we were all legal!

In between their Lotus commitments drivers would compete in all types of machinery. Jackie Oliver, while racing the F2 Lotus 48 sponsored by the Herts and Essex Aero Club, took time out to compete in a 105E Anglia for Chris Craft Racing. He managed to roll it several times and was fortunate to escape with minor injuries. Shortly after, he paid a visit to my home, but I was out. The babysitter opened the door and screamed when she saw Jackie standing there with red bloodshot eyes!

One of our development engineers was John Joyce. He was a good designer, but once, while completing a car for testing on the works track it became obvious to us while still working at 2am that the driveshafts would clash with the springs on the dampers. Unable to find a way around this problem I phoned John at his home. He said he had lots of ideas of how to solve the problem, but when I asked what they were he answered, "I haven't thought of them yet." He did come into the workshop and succeeded in finding a solution so that we could test later in the day.

John eventually returned to his native Australia, but before he went he managed to acquire a space frame Formula Ford chassis which he cut in half to reduce the crate size before sending it off in many packages to various airfields in Australia to avoid paying import duty. In later years he designed the successful Bowin Formula Ford.

Another development engineer (who shall remain nameless!) made a big error of judgement when he removed a brake pad from a prepared test car to check some measurements and failed to put it back. Unaware that this had happened, we lowered the car off its trolley and sent John Miles out for a test run. We only realised something was wrong when John returned shortly after and was none too happy to find that he had little braking power. Just as well he hadn't gone out onto the main Hethel circuit.

Several of the workforce at Hethel were engineers on a smaller scale. One such was fabricator Jim Bamber, who sat at his bench every lunchtime building a model steam traction engine. The wheels of this were approximately ten inches in diameter, and he replicated every minute detail including making tiny studs to fit on the wheel rims. He worked on this for several years. I often wonder if he ever completed it.

Jim Bamber and the Thorne brothers built Scalextric racing car models and Colin allowed them to build a large racetrack – complete with flyover and pits – in the old control tower used by the Americans during the war. Graham Hill and Jim Clark would pop in to have a (smaller scale) race. Other Scalextric clubs were sometimes invited to come along and compete.

During 1969 and 1970 we built the Dave Baldwin designed type 59 and 69, in a small area of the Components workshop under the name of Lotus Racing. These were for F2 and F3 and were of a spaceframe design.

The first race of the F2 season was at Thruxton over the Easter weekend, and it was always a panic to finish the cars in the amount of time given. They arrived very late,

A works type 59 at Cadwell Park. From left to right; Myself, Dave Baldwin, Alan Beaton, Francois Mazet (driver), Jim Pickles and Colin Bennett

after working all night, without ever turning a wheel, but Rindt managed to win the 1969 race despite starting way down the grid due to some minor issues. In 1970, he won from pole position. He wasn't called the 'King of F2' for nothing. The cars were run by Roy Winkelmann Racing and Jochen was managed by none other than Bernie Ecclestone, who was none too happy that they arrived late! He came up to the factory whilst we were building them to vent his anger!

At this point it's worth mentioning the introduction of wings – an unknown area at that time. The early wings were high up above the car in the clean air, and attached to the rear uprights. In theory this seemed to be an ideal set up, but no one understood the amount of downforce they created, and a vast majority buckled or fell off causing several accidents. Later, adjustable wings front and rear were developed and all teams used a variety of methods to adjust these from the cockpit, including hydraulics, a foot pedal, electrics and counterweights etc... As these all caused many problems and accidents the FIA banned adjustable wings completely. The wings remained, but the regulations stated they had to be mounted lower for safety. Colin devised a strut with rubber inserted to allow the wing to run flat at high speed and elevate at slow speed, but this was thrown out by the officials (good try though!). Most of the teams had aeroplanes, but did not realise the potential of aerodynamics. Years later, the addition of side skirts that remained in contact with the track creating ground-effects also caused more problems. Many more aerodynamic changes would come in the future.

Jochen Rindt won at Thruxton in 1970 in an F2 type 69 I built in the corner of the Components factory. By that time, we were Lotus Racing.

One of the most interesting projects I worked on – although in a small way – was the turbine-engined 56B F1 car. In my opinion, this was a frightening race car. When starting it up in the yard, with Dick Scammell in the cockpit, his foot would be hard down on the brake pedal, and we had chocks under the wheels to restrain it. The engine would start to wind up, giving a roar from the exhaust (funnel) not unlike a Boeing 707! The car was raced by John Miles, Reine Wisell, Emerson Fittipaldi, Jochen Rindt and Dave Walker. John, when testing the car at Hethel, told us there was no 'feel through the pants' as with a conventional racing car, as the turbine ran quieter and, with a delay in the turbine response of about two seconds, it made it difficult to drive, especially in corners. The weight of the car and power of the turbine meant that brake pads didn't last very long, and thicker ones had to be specially made. Other competitors complained that the heat haze from the engine made visibility exceedingly difficult when passing. Overall, a nightmare car to race.

The original type 72 had a three-plane rear wing set up, and after a test session we found a mark on the lower plane as it had flexed and touched an oil cooler mounted about four inches below. Colin suggested putting sand bags on the wing to see how much downforce had been created and we were all amazed.

We built a type 70 for Formula 5000, which was designed by Martin Waide. Alan Rollinson was due to race it at Brands Hatch, but unfortunately it grounded on an uneven part of the track caused by a tree root and the rear end was torn off. Many years later while attending the funeral of Eddie Dennis, one of the longest-serving members of Team Lotus, I was speaking to Martin and he told me that according to John Miles the sump of the Chevrolet engine was an inch and a half lower than the chassis, thus causing the accident.

We built a replacement second car for our Australian works driver, Dave Walker. We finished it around midnight, but as Dave was due to arrive and test it the next day we

The selection of cars for display at the 1971 Racing Car Show await collection from Hethel. Left to right; John Lambert, me, Derek Brooks and Peter Brand.

1971

had to check it all worked. Starting up the V8 engine, that we were told had only just come off the test bed, proved a problem, so we towed it out onto the dark test circuit to try and get it running. While I sat in the driver's seat our little yellow Morris pick up towed the car down the straight with sheets of flame coming out of the inlet trumpets, lighting up the faces of the mechanics sat in the back of the pick-up. We returned to the workshop and successfully re-timed the engine before I set off again onto the straight part of the circuit, with cars at either end guiding me with their headlights as I went back and forth between them. This was a frightening car for me to drive, and with only minor throttle applied it would soon lose the back end, so actual testing was left to Dave Walker.

A few of these cars were built and the Scottish driver Jock Russell raced one in the UK. Years later this car was rebuilt by the renowned restorer of Lotus race cars, Peter Denty, complete with tartan seat cover! Before it was tested at Snetterton he dropped in to Van Diemen's, where I was working at the time, to show me the car. As always with Peter's cars it looked better than the original.

I did some work on the prototype Lotus Europa sports car, which had a Renault engine and gearbox with the development number of P5. John Joyce and I took it to Silverstone to drive up and down the inner runways, enabling us to check that all the components were working. I was giving this 'roller skate' (so called because it lacked bodywork at this stage) plenty of 'welly' when I completely lost control and spun several times just as Colin Chapman happened to be flying over the runway. Later he asked who the f*** was driving P5? I owned up and he just laughed – what a relief.

Colin had flown in to oversee the testing and check on the lap times of the F3 car. He decided to try the car for himself and once out on the track he couldn't be persuaded to come back in. Eventually, he ran out of fuel. He thoroughly enjoyed it and was a brilliant driver, sometimes testing cars faster than regular drivers. I remember once, Innes Ireland was complaining that his car wasn't handling well, so Colin took it out for a few laps and equalled his time, saying there was nothing wrong with it.

After his drive in the F3 car Colin decide to leave while John Joyce and myself (as a passenger this time) took P5 for another trial down the runway doing around 70mph. Imagine our horror when we saw Colin hurtling towards us in his light aircraft! John took evasive action and we ended up in a cabbage field, with luckily no damage to man or machine. I'm sure Colin enjoyed the moment!

Putting the finishing touches to a F2 type 69.
© Eastern Daily Press *(Norwich)*.

Talking with David Coulthard when he drove Jimmy's type 25 at Silverstone in 2013.

"During my years with Team Lotus there were as many as 28 Formula One races in a single season, the majority of which were non-championship. It was logistically impossible for me to attend all of them, but I did attend more than I missed."

8

CIRCUIT TALES – PART THREE
UK

During my years with Team Lotus there were as many as 28 Formula One races in a single season, the majority of which were non-championship. It was logistically impossible for me to attend all of them, but I did attend more than I missed.

From the previous pages you will have gathered that everything was transported via road and ferry whenever possible. It wouldn't be unusual to work one or even two all-nighters with no break, then drive the transporter hundreds of miles across Europe, changing drivers without stopping by slipping from the passenger to the driver's seat and vice versa, all to save precious minutes. When competing outside of Europe the cars and equipment would be flown out of Heathrow Airport. It was always quite a sight seeing all the cars from the various teams waiting to be loaded onto a Boeing 707 cargo plane.

As an example of the punishing schedule in 1963 – when Jimmy won the world championship – he competed in 20 F1 races, ten of which were non-championship.

30th March – Snetterton (non-championship)
15th April – Pau (non-championship)
21st April – Imola (non-championship)
27th April – Aintree (non-championship)
11th May – Silverstone (non-championship)
26th May – Monaco

9th June – Spa-Francorchamps
23rd June – Zandvoort
30th June – Reims
20th July – Silverstone
28th July – Solitude (non-championship)
4th August – Nürburgring
11th August – Karlskoga (non-championship)
1st September – Zeltweg (non-championship)
8th September – Monza
21st September – Oulton Park (non-championship)
6th October – Watkins Glen
27th October – Mexico City
14th December – Kyalami (non-championship)
28th December – East London

The following – in no particular order or preference – are some of the memories, escapades and memorable races that occurred at the many circuits in the UK, which I was fortunate to visit during my days involved with Team Lotus.

AINTREE

More famous for its horse racing – in particularly, the Grand National – Aintree was situated on the outskirts of Liverpool and was owned at the time by Mrs Topham.

When Jim Clark was driving to one of the meetings he

was stopped by the police for exceeding the speed limit in his Lotus Elan. They asked, "Who do you think you are – Jim Clark?"! On his passport his occupation was listed as a farmer.

At one of the meetings there was a combined race for F1/F2 cars. Jimmy was following Jack Brabham closely until Jack overtook the F2 car of Jo Schlesser, who immediately dropped in behind Jack for a tow, not realising that Jimmy was there. Jimmy went off the track, through some straw bales and into a brick hut, severely damaging the brand-new Lotus we had just finished after many hours of hard labour. Photographs later showed that, as he was going off the circuit towards the hut, he slid down in the cockpit and just the top of his helmet was visible. No seat belts then, of course.

In the 1963 Aintree 200, Jimmy's car would not start on the grid, so he held up his hand to alert the other drivers who luckily managed to avoid him. After a battery change in the pits he set off and began making up ground, but was several laps behind. Colin (Chapman) decided to bring in Trevor Taylor on lap 18, so Jimmy could take over his car. With some foam padding shoved down behind his back, he rejoined the race lapping 1.5 seconds quicker than Trevor and eventually made it up to third place, while Trevor, now in Jimmy's car, came home seventh, three laps down. It was a tremendous feat to watch and showed Jimmy's true talent.

OULTON PARK

Set in the grounds of Oulton Hall, Cheshire, this attractive British circuit was the venue for the F1 International Gold Cup. The race would be over 70+ laps, a distance of over 200 miles, which proved a real challenge due to its undulating nature, blind crests and some quick corners with little run-off. One of the most demanding corners

was Knickerbrook, so named after Buster Bates' tales of demolition in the area. Apparently, after he had used explosives on an old building, he saw a young couple running away very distressed, only to later recover a pair of ladies' knickers!

Jimmy won the Gold Cup in 1962 and 1963, while Stirling Moss in a Rob Walker-entered Lotus 18 won it in 1960.

SILVERSTONE

This Northamptonshire circuit owned by the British Racing Drivers' Club (BRDC) was until 1948 an RAF airfield, which meant that it was usually cold and windy. Many corners had railway sleepers around the edge of the grass and run off areas. The inner runway was used as the paddock area and was a long walk from the toilets and water supply, but gave plenty of space for transporters and, if necessary, room to tow start the cars. When holding out signalling boards to the drivers caution had to be taken when crossing the pit lane as cars could be coming into the pits at full speed (no speed regulations then!). One mechanic's signal board he was carrying was caught by the rear wheel of an incoming car, which spun him round like a spinning top. He was then taken off to the St John Ambulance station and practice continued.

We usually stayed at a small hotel near the circuit owned by Mr Pearson, who raced Jaguars. One evening, while we sat waiting for our meal, there was an almighty noise in the kitchen. We rushed through to find, not only Mrs Pearson covered in cabbage, but also the whole room – including the walls – as the pressure cooker had exploded! While Mr Pearson took his wife off for a check-up, we ended up in the local Towcester chippy.

I remember on the road from Towcester to Silverstone there was a small copse, where we used to wave to an old

I'm driving Jimmy's type 25 from the paddock (the old runway) at the Grand Prix in 1963.
© Peter Denty.

tramp sitting by his fire with his makeshift shelter. He was there for several years and always stayed in my memories of Silverstone.

The small lanes leading to the track always made getting in and out extremely difficult and we always had to queue. One year, Trevor Taylor had a shunt in practice and we drove the Bedford transporter back to Cheshunt to rebuild his car in time for the race the next day. We worked all night and then headed back to the circuit in the early morning, but massive queues were already forming some distance away. We were becoming very anxious as to whether or not we would make it in time, so decided we had no choice but to drive up the right-hand side of

Team mechanic and Elan driver, Ray Parsons, testing the Tasman car in 1966, before it was shipped over to compete in the series down under.

Left to right; Myself, Bill Cowe, Bob Dance, Cedric Selzer and the official Team photographer Peter Darley, when David Coulthard drove Jimmy's type 25.

Jimmy testing the type 38 Indy car

the road for a while. This we did until a police motorcycle rider came along and escorted us to the paddock just in time for the race.

In 1963, we raced there with Jim Clark and Trevor Taylor. During practice Jim came into the pits for a rear wheel change, so the car was raised on the quick lift jack. We used a speed brace as our Lotus 'Wobbly Web' wheels were secured by six brass (Austin Seven) nuts and these were pinched tight, ready to be tightened on the ground, but as soon as the car was lowered Colin told Jim to "GO!"

We had a big panic to get Jim in again on the next lap, and heated words followed, ending in an apology from Colin later. Jim won the race, and afterwards a lone Scottish bagpiper played "Scotland the Brave" for Jim and his supporters. This sometimes occurred at other race meetings featuring Jim, and was always appreciated by everyone.

BRM had arranged to loan their third Type 578 to the Italian team Scuderia Centro-Sud for Lorenzo Bandini. It had been painted red and was run by BRM mechanic, Arthur Hill. Bandini finished fifth but was disqualified for a push start. After the race the car was transported on an open back truck and driven by the always jovial Arthur. As we left the circuit we were side by side in the queue to reach the exit – us being in the Team Lotus Bedford transporter. As we reached the lane Arthur decided to cut across in front of us, misjudged it and ending up taking off the front of our transporter. This had to be rebuilt at great cost, so not a good end to a successful day.

In 2013, I was invited, along with my fellow Lotus 25 mechanics, Cedric Selzer and Billy Cowe, to Silverstone to see David Coulthard drive Jim's Lotus 25, which was a Classic Team Lotus car and was taken there by Bob Dance. David put on a fantastic display and said how great it was to drive it. There were several photographers present, including the Lotus photographer Peter Darley. We were interviewed and had photos taken with David.

GOODWOOD

It was always a pleasure to go to Goodwood, one of our best and most historic circuits situated in Sussex. All the famous names had competed there, including Fangio, Ascari, Hawthorn, Brooks, Moss and Gonzalez.

It was a fine circuit – fast and flowing with a very tight chicane, which once caught out Jean Behra in his BRM. There is a much-publicised photo of him being somersaulted out of the cockpit. It's probably best known for being the track at which Stirling Moss crashed in 1962, driving a BRP Lotus 24. He was trapped in the cockpit for 40 minutes and was very seriously injured. He returned to Goodwood a year later to see if he was confident enough to resume his racing career. Unfortunately, while his times were reasonable, his concentration wasn't, so he decided to retire at 37 years-old. A sad loss to motor racing.

There were two non-championship F1 races held there in 1960 and 1961. We often tested at Goodwood and took the Lotus F. Junior for Jimmy to try, but it rained very heavily and the track was saturated, so impossible to test. Jimmy had driven down in his Lotus Elan and invited me to go with him on a few 'fun' laps. Heading towards the first corner flat out, with the wipers full on, I was convinced I was going to die, but with a flick of the wrist we slid through the corner. His driving skills were superb and it was a tremendous thrill to be driven by him. Afterwards he chuckled at my early tenseness.

The canteen was a very friendly place, with decent food. The staff told us that many celebrities kept their small aeroplanes there, including the comedian Jimmy Edwards, who apparently once chased the groundsman along the runway with his aircraft.

In October 2013, I was invited, along with some former colleagues, by Lord March to The Jim Clark Goodwood Revival Tribute. All of his cars were there and driven round the circuit by various retired 'old' racing drivers, including Stirling Moss, Tony Brooks and John Surtees. Lord March gave a presentation speech at which several F1 drivers were present. It shows just how much respect Jimmy is held in.

BRANDS HATCH

Having started life as a motorcycle grass track, it was gradually transformed into one of Britain's premier circuits. The first section – the 'Indy' circuit – is in a natural bowl and provides excellent viewing for spectators, who can almost see the circuit in its entirety.

The Grand Prix was first held there in 1964 on the longer 2.65-mile GP layout and had the grand title of the Royal Automobile Club (RAC) British Grand Prix sponsored by the *Daily Mail*.

There were many demonstrations/attractions before the main event. The Band of the Royal Dragoons and Battalion of the Royal Scots were followed by a mock battle using helicopters, scout cars and troops. This caused mayhem when the downdraught from the helicopters blew all the merchandise off the temporary stalls up into the air! All this took place on the grass area in the middle of the track, which meant the public had a good view. The salute was taken by Earl Mountbatten of Burma.

One of the less formal attractions – unbeknown to us – was a topless model posing on the top of a sports car in the paddock. I was made aware of it by the ex-motorcycle racer, and now privateer F1 driver, Bob Anderson, when I was walking down the paddock with a watering can. He said, "Quick, get on my shoulders." This enabled me to see what was causing the excitement – the car was nice too!

Another incident wasn't quite as entertaining, when I had to take Jim Endruweit's Ford Cortina to pick Colin up, who had landed his aeroplane in a sloping field near the circuit. The driver's seat had broken, which made driving

Hanging out the signalling board for Jimmy at the 1964 Grand Prix. Dick Scammell is alongside with the stopwatch. ©Esso Petroleum

The victory parade. © Associated Newspapers

difficult. I was sliding about and the only way I could stop was to hold the steering column to steady myself. Colin asked, "What the **** are you doing?" This was a sort of payback for the time abroad when he was sitting behind me in a car full of mechanics. He suddenly tipped my seat forward, putting my nose up against the windscreen!

The paddock was a makeshift affair with structures made from scaffolding with corrugated roof panels. They did provide shelter, but left very little room to work. Luckily, we had good weather.

To get to the pits the cars had to be driven through a very narrow single-track tunnel under the top of Paddock Hill Bend. The narrowness made it exceedingly difficult to manoeuvre them, as a BRM mechanic found out when attempting to take Graham Hill's car through for practice.

He misjudged how wide the rear was and tore off a rear corner on a scaffolding pole. Graham was not amused and had to do first practice in the spare car. All this amused us and the other teams, apart from BRM of course.

By qualifying in pole position, Jimmy won 100 bottles of champagne, courtesy of the *Evening News*. Dan Gurney in his Brabham had won the same for being fastest in first practice.

The race was run in dry, overcast conditions, saw Jimmy battling with Graham and John Surtees for much of it, with Jimmy coming out on top. The winning car was put onto the back of a lorry along with Jimmy, Colin, myself and fellow mechanics, and was driven around the circuit for the benefit of the thousands of fans who had attended this memorable race.

A rare quiet moment during a Grand Prix weekend.

Early testing of the prototype type 41. That's my Cortina GT in the background.

SNETTERTON

Often cold and windy, the circuit was originally an airfield used by the American 96th Bombardment Group in the Second World War. The paddock was small, the washing facilities poor, some first aid equipment was stored in the timing tower, the pit area had some small lock-up garages and only the one ambulance would be parked nearby. All in all, pretty basic. On a positive note, the clubhouse and bar were good and always stayed open late.

Upon arrival we had to book in at a small bungalow and drive down to the paddock to be greeted by the manager, who always seemed more interested in hunting, shooting and fishing, than in racing cars, and would often wander off around the area with his shotgun looking for game for his larder – although he did run an immaculate Alvis convertible. The only other person around would be the St John Ambulance lady, who also made a lovely cup of tea.

To fuel the cars up we had to drive down the long straight alongside the main A11 London to Norwich Road, to the Esso station that served both track and main road customers. Fred Bowers was the well-known, friendly

Station Manager, assisted by Shane Woodroffe. I got to know the pair very well as we used to test on a regular basis when we were based in Cheshunt, and later when we moved to Hethel. Due to the long straight running parallel with the aforementioned main road it caused quite a few accidents, as drivers were watching the racing cars instead of the road. Another issue was, if drivers overshot the tight hairpin and mounted the banking they came close to ending up in the resident hot dog van; just two of the reasons why the circuit was shortened by removing that section for safety reasons. The changes did make it difficult to fuel up the cars, so we either used a small Esso tanker in the paddock or used the fuel we carried in the transporter.

A benefit of arriving early was the chance to do a few laps warming up the engines and checking the systems, which was great fun! Less fun was the time when we were having problems with a Lotus 23. I had to crouch in the small passenger area, bracing myself and spreading my weight on the thin fibreglass undertray, to see if there were any air bubbles in the fuel going through the transparent plastic pipe. Not such a good experience at 100mph, and facing backwards! I'd like to think this might qualify for a world record. Peter Arundell, who was behind the wheel, thought it was all highly amusing.

On a rare visit as a spectator I travelled up in my Ford Anglia 100E and was passed by a rapid Archie Scott-Brown in a Lister Jaguar. A little while later I saw it parked by the roadside with a jack underneath and a wheel off. He did eventually make it in time to race, and as always put on a good show despite his disability of only having one good hand.

A non-championship F1 race was held in March, 1964, and was for the *Daily Mirror* Trophy. Unfortunately, both our cars retired – Jimmy with electrical problems, while Peter (Arundell) spun off and damaged the water system. We had worked on the cars at J.J. Wright, the Ford main dealers, and stayed at The George – a friendly pub with good food. Both were in the nearby market town of East Dereham.

We loaded up the cars after the race and Peter offered me a lift back to London in his Mini-Cooper, which I gladly accepted as it meant I would get home about five hours quicker than in the transporter. The meeting was still going on, but in between the races we drove around the circuit and went down a dust track that took us to the main road – it was a shortcut known to Peter. He drove like he was still racing, through heavy traffic – obviously still full of adrenalin. During the journey we came up behind Paddy Hopkirk in his Mini-Cooper (Paddy built and rallied Minis) and from then on the rest of the drive, or should that be race, back to the capital was exhilarating. Eventually, I bought the car (registration 00 4600) from Peter, and ran it for a couple of years before selling it – one of the few regrets in my life, along with selling my Lotus Seven and Austin-Healey.

It wasn't unusual to have two F2 races on the same weekend, and normally they would be in the same country, but over the Easter holidays in 1968 with Jackie Oliver and the type 48, we raced at Zandvoort and Snetterton, which meant a tight schedule. I managed to spend a couple of hours

The Mini I bought from Peter Arundell.

preparing the car while the public were leaving the circuit, as it was difficult to leave at the same time. We then loaded up and headed for the ferry. I needed to change the gearbox ratios for the Snetterton race and thought that, if I could get down to the transporter on the lower deck, I would have plenty of time to do the work – so persuaded an officer to let me onto the lower deck. I started to work in the very cramped area at the back of our transporter, but unfortunately there was quite a swell on the sea and, along with the vibration of the ship's engines and the petrol fumes, I only just managed to finish. I dashed up to the top deck for some much-needed fresh air, before being violently ill. On route to the circuit we were delayed by the crowd of people queuing to attend a horse racing event at Newmarket and only just made it in time for practice. All in all, a stressful and hectic weekend.

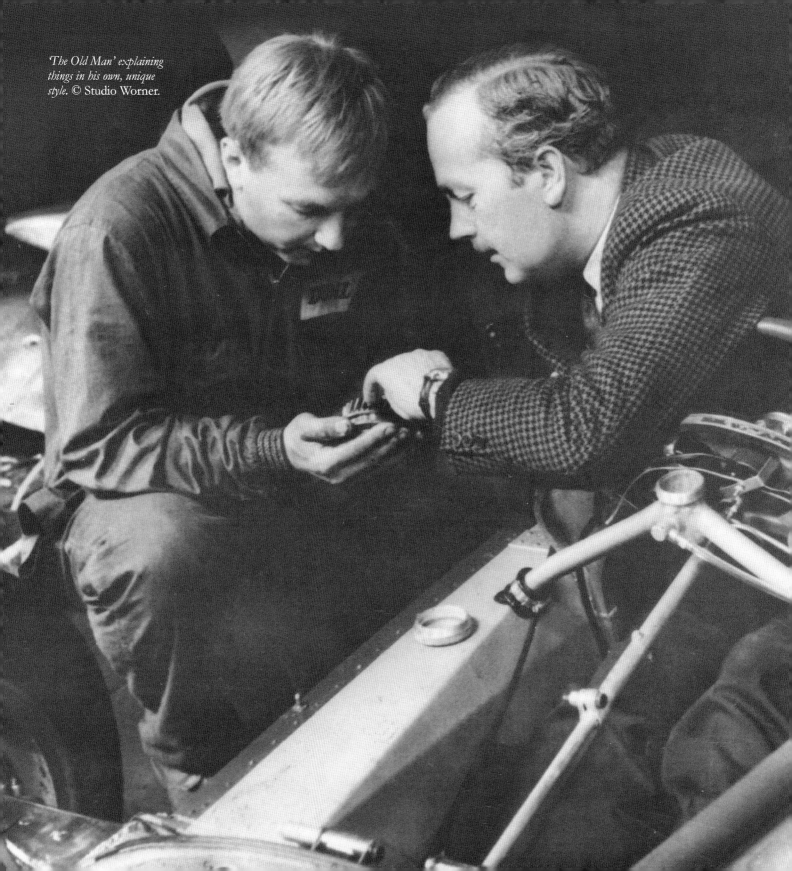

'The Old Man' explaining things in his own, unique style. © Studio Worner.

9

MEMORABLE LOTUS PEOPLE

I must start with the person who gave me the opportunity to pursue a career in motor sport, **Jim Endruweit**, who interviewed me early in 1960.

Jim joined Lotus in 1958, and held many positions: F1 Chief Mechanic (his role when he interviewed me), Engineering Director and finally, Service Director. The last position was not one Jim enjoyed, so he returned to his original trade of aircraft engineering, working at Norwich Airport. He also covered other aspects of Team Lotus, including the Indianapolis races.

You could tell Jim apart from the rest of us by his distinctive slip-on shoes/white socks combination. He enjoyed smoking the French Gauloises brand, several packs of which were brought back from France via the Team Lotus truck.

Jim was a very calm man who never lost his temper, even when under extreme pressure from Colin. His enthusiasm for getting the work finished to a high standard was always his goal and spurred us all on. We couldn't have had a better or more thoughtful leader translating Colin's ideas and instructions into a workable programme.

The next obvious person is of course the top man, **Colin Chapman CBE**, or to use his full name, Anthony Colin Bruce Chapman. His initials (ACBC) are featured on the Lotus badge. Depending on the situation he was also known as 'Chunky', 'The Governor' or 'The Old Man'.

Colin was the inspiration for many designers and engineers to start their own businesses all over Britain. His

> *Jim was a very calm man who never lost his temper, even when under extreme pressure from Colin. His enthusiasm for getting the work finished to a high standard was always his goal and spurred us all on.*

amazing forward vision and technical abilities inspired us mechanics to work night and day to try and achieve his desires, although things didn't always go to plan. While I admired him and his total commitment to motorsport, he wasn't always the easiest person to work for as I have highlighted on a few occasions in previous chapters. No problem was 'unsolvable' in his mind, which made our job at times a little stressful. At the end of a practice session he would often produce a job list of approximately 100 modifications to be completed before practice the next day, while he would depart with Jimmy and try to persuade him to change the set-up of the car. If he was successful this would be relayed to us during the evening if we were lucky, or if we were less fortunate the next morning. The latter wasn't always the best move to make. While other teams would finish late in the evening, we would still be working through the job list well into the small hours and, on occasion, through the night making and fitting new parts.

Colin was obsessed with the weight of the cars and one of his favourite sayings was "Add lightness to the

Cheshunt 1963, Colin Riley, and a type 25. Behind is the 105E left-hand drive, twin-cam test car, which 'The Governor' encountered on the M1.

car." This would often entail removing parts like flat washers, etc... and cutting off the excess threads from bolts. Another area was the amount of fuel the cars raced with. He would calculate how much fuel we added with the possibility of running out on the slowing down lap, thus keeping the car as light as possible. Sometimes his calculations were a bit marginal, to say the least. With the Chief Mechanic's approval we often added a 'mechanic's gallon' for some extra security. If Colin had known about this he would have blown his top.

He was a law unto himself and never let authority phase him. I remember taking his Jaguar to Panshanger aerodrome – a Lotus storage area – to meet him when he flew in. He was an hour late, so being inquisitive I fiddled with the controls of the car for a while before peering into the glove box. To my amazement scores of speeding tickets fell out – none of which had been dealt with. Such was the man – there were more important things in life.

When flying to the States, if he was late, he would pull up, leap out of the car with his briefcase and holdall, and run off into the airport leaving the car door open and engine running. The authorities would put it in a compound and Colin would pay a fine when collecting it upon his return.

He would tell us stories of his earlier pre-Lotus days, while working as a draughtsman for the Metal Box Company. The evenings were spent preparing his sports car, and if racing in France over the weekend, he would leave very early on Friday with the car on a trailer to catch the boat. If he had problems in practice he would overcome them by making parts from road signs/fences, etc... so he could race on Sunday. Having sailed back on the midnight ferry he would be back, washed and shaved, but very tired at his drawing board on Monday at 8.30am. By lunchtime he would be asleep. His fellow workers would often leave him, but one day his boss walked in and found him. This was the signal to move on and to start building cars professionally.

Another story relayed to us was when he was going up the M1 in his Jaguar, doing over 90mph in atrocious weather, and he could see a ball of spray ahead. When he came up behind he realised it was Steve Sanville, our engine shop chief, in the Lotus twin-cam 105E left-hand drive engine development car. This surprised him, but it was a necessary test drive.

These glimpses into his life that we sometimes shared helped us to understand the man we worked tirelessly for, and indeed why we were prepared to do it. His untimely death in 1982 was a great loss to motorsport, and the epitaph on his gravestone says it all – CRESCIT SUB PONDERE VIRTUS (In adversity we thrive)

Another extremely dedicated person was **Andrew Ferguson**, who originally worked for Coopers. He worked as the Competitions Manager from 1961 – 1969, and was essentially Colin's right-hand man. At one stage, Andrew lived on a new estate (on which, after his advice, I also purchased a property). With no telephone line yet installed in the house he took himself off to a nearby phone box, complete with stool/coffee/torch/warm clothes (it was February) and a bag full of coins to chase up the delivery of ZF gearboxes, which after many phone calls were found to be on a train stuck in a snowdrift in Germany. This method of contact was used by him on several occasions.

He was a man of fantastic character, and no problem was too big for him to solve. He always seemed to have a smile on his face, even when under severe stress, especially during negotiations sorting out the team's participation at Indianapolis. He later returned to Lotus in 1976 and ran Club Team Lotus, was the team archivist and produced a magazine for Lotus enthusiasts until his death in 1994.

Mike Warner joined Lotus at Hethel and took over the running of Lotus Components, who were responsible for the building of all customer single-seater and sports cars, including the special 47 road going promotion car with a Rover V8 engine and cream leather trim for GKN (the huge car parts manufacturer).

In his contract it stated that, after leaving, he wasn't allowed to participate in any other motor racing projects for one year. After many heated discussions with Colin over various things, including Colin's decision to end the production of customer racing cars in early 1971, he resigned. I was made redundant, so along with my former colleagues, Gordon Huckle and Dave Baldwin, we linked up with Mike to form Group Racing Developments (GRD) in late 1971. As Mike had shares in Griston Engineering we used their premises to start production. Colin was aware of this so sent a security guard to watch the premises, ensuring that Mike didn't go there. To avoid any problems we had meetings at his home or late at night. We always gave the guard a wave as we were working to let him know we were aware of him. The GRD badge was a phoenix rising from the ashes, with the motto 'Camaraderie' – a poignant reminder of what had been.

We were very successful in our first season (1972), much to Colin's surprise and annoyance.

Sales Director **Graham Arnold** was keen to push the sales of the Lotus 61 Formula Ford that was being built at the time, causing a dispute over production numbers between him and Mike (Warner), so they were both called into Colin's office, and after a hectic discussion Graham said to Colin he could sell as many cars as Mike could build. This was like a red rag to a bull as far as Mike was concerned, and Lotus Components/Racing went on to build 248 of the wedge-shaped Formula Fords. In fact, they built so many they were stacked in all the old hangars around Hethel, giving Graham many anxious moments selling them!

It's worth mentioning that in later years Graham 'fell foul of the law' and served a period at Her Majesty's Pleasure. On his release he was picked up by Ted Savory (Modus Racing), who landed his helicopter in the prison car park – quite an exit!

We worked with people from all walks of life, but one that stands out in my memory was **Arthur Hobern**, who was the engineer responsible for the building of gearboxes. In his own time he would occasionally work on Ferrari and Maserati transmissions. He was a very talented engineer. Before joining Lotus he and his wife spent many years travelling the world with a circus. Arthur was a lion tamer, while his wife was an acrobat, and also proficient at riding a one-wheeled cycle.

The circus was transported via rail and truck, which gave Arthur the opportunity to make a little extra cash by dealing in illegal alcohol and cigarettes. These he would store in the lion's cage under the straw covering, safe in the knowledge that no customs official would dare to inspect that area!

Ron Buxton was another more senior in years production fitter, with the most fantastic memory. He built the Type 23 sports cars and could inform us of all the parts on the car, including bolt lengths, sizes, threads, etc... There was a 23 at Tilbury Docks that had the screen broken by someone climbing into the driver's seat, so I drove Ron down to replace it. On the way through London he pointed out all the historical places and gave me detailed information on them. He was a real motoring enthusiast and kept all his magazines in one room of his house. He once informed a Bentley owner the history of his car by knowing the exact number of spokes in the wheels.

Nick Parravani worked in the Hethel panel and fabrication workshop, learning quickly from the experienced staff to become one of the finest craftsmen Lotus ever produced – and I have ever seen – in the motor industry. He joined us at GRD, and later started his own business in Norfolk rebuilding all types of racing and vintage cars and motor-cycles. He has rebuilt cars from the sixties that I originally worked on. **Peter Denty**, another Lotus employee, also went on to do a similar thing in Norfolk, working on restoring cars to a very high standard. He would often call in to see me at Van Diemen's and show them to me on his way to Snetterton for testing.

Australian **Ray Parsons** was mechanic to Peter Arundell and also raced the Team 26R Lotus Elan. When Peter was late arriving for practice in Sweden, Ray put on Peter's overalls and distinctive red helmet and proceeded to take the Lotus Formula Junior round the track, earning Peter a respectable place on the grid – something unheard of in racing today. He tested Jim Clark's Tasman car and later went out to New Zealand for the races with him as his mechanic.

Nick Folliard worked with us at Cheshunt, and later Hethel, in the development department. While working at Cheshunt he owned a DKW and an early-type Porsche. A customer arrived from Europe with a trailer on which appeared to be a Lotus 23 under a tarpaulin, but when this was removed it was the remains of a DKW, with a few metal hoops welded to it to form a 23 shape. We then replaced it all with a new Lotus 23 and he drove off to go back through customs with his 'repaired' 23, thus saving him from paying customs duty. Nick then swiftly removed the DKW remains to take as spares. He later went on to form his own hydraulics business, and still occasionally works with the McLaren, Mercedes and Red Bull F1 teams making test equipment and systems for the hydraulics on their cars. A very talented, experienced and sought-after engineer.

I must include a very familiar name to many – **Bob Dance**. He arrived for his interview in 1960 driving a 750cc Austin Dante home-built sports car. He started in the engine shop and had the job of making the F1 Colotti gearboxes work properly when they arrived from Italy. He then went on to work with all Team Lotus cars and was Chief Mechanic on the works Cortinas. We nicknamed him 'Bob Lotti' when he worked on the Italian Colotti gearboxes – a good design but with poor finishing on the gears – and later 'The Vicar', due to his love of a cup of tea! He must be the longest serving team member, and is still participating in events at the time of writing (2024).

The early workforce included some fantastically brilliant designers, especially **Mike Costin**, who was in charge of the Design Department (he would leave and join up with Keith Duckworth to form Cosworth Engineering). **Len Terry**, who designed many Lotus models and Indianapolis cars (he later joined Dan Gurney and his All American Racing Team). **Ron Hickman**, who designed the famous Elan Plus 2. He went on to design the popular Workmate that most of us now have in our workshops and garages. He later sold the production rights to Black and Decker, which made him a tidy fortune, before moving to live in Jersey. **David Baldwin**, who was responsible for the 59 and 69 F2/F3 cars before joining us at GRD. He did some freelance F1 work for Mo Nunn at Ensign – his N176 design was very competitive in the hands of Chris Amon – and the Fittipaldi team. He's probably most

Some of the memorable people I worked with. Left to right; Ian Seymour, Bill Cowe, Jim Endruweit, me, Nick Garbett (partially obscured), John 'The Gear' (can't remember his surname), Colin Riley, Dick Scammell, and Doug Bridge. We assembled for the photo when the great Fangio dropped in for a visit. It wasn't unusual for drivers to pop in for a look around.

famous for his highly successful designs for Van Diemen stretching to well over thirty years. **Geoff Aldridge** was another great designer, who later teamed up with David (Baldwin) at Van Diemen. **Bill Wells** made the move with us from Cheshunt to Hethel and worked for many years. He was a draughtsman/designer, who in his spare time would make wooden gear lever knobs of many shapes and designs, selling them to Lotus and other car manufacturers. This 'side-line' eventually took off so well that he left

Lotus and made this his main business. Initially, the wood he used came from old rifle butts purchased from the M.O.D. He continued to make wooden parts for Lotus at his own factory, and went on to make television stands for rental companies. He was a keen sub-aqua diver and pilot of his own aeroplane.

The above are a small selection of the many talented Lotus people I have worked with. To list them all would be impossible. My apologies to those I have omitted to mention.

I consider myself fortunate to have worked with the greatest of all time. © Marius Garb *(East London)*

"Jim was a humble, shy and polite man with a great
sense of humour. His talent was beyond belief."

10
LOTUS DRIVERS I WORKED WITH

The first driver whose car I looked after was **Innes Ireland**, and his works 2½ litre Coventry Climax FPF Lotus 18. This car had to be push started and Innes would keep his foot hard down on the throttle pedal, so when the engine fired up the car would rapidly accelerate away, leaving some unwary pushers falling flat on their faces. He left Lotus at the end of the 1961 season and was replaced by Jim Clark, which was a very controversial decision at the time and one Innes was less than happy about.

In those days – logistically, with the number of races – I would work on both of the team's race cars. The next two drivers I had the pleasure of working with were **Jim Clark** and **Trevor Taylor**.

Jim was a Scottish farmer with a love of motorsport, and for a while would drive home after his races in a silver Porsche 356 to continue farming, before racing took over his life. The other cars Jim had during my time working with him were a Lotus Elan and a Lotus Cortina loaned by Chapman, fitted with independent rear suspension with a view to Lotus producing the car with that modification, but the Ford Motor Company didn't grant their approval.

His driving ability was recognised and encouraged by Ian Scott-Watson, whose cars he drove for a while before progressing to the Border Reivers, a team local to him in the Scottish Borders. His performances in their D-type earned him a test in a type 16 at Brands Hatch. It was his first time in a single-seater and his lap times impressed a watching Colin Chapman. He further impressed Colin on Boxing Day, 1958, at Brands Hatch, in Scott-Watson's brand-new Lotus Elite. They were both in Elites and Jim stayed ahead of Colin – a very competent racer in his own right – until he fell foul of a backmarker and Colin sneaked past to claim the win. The rest, as they say, is history.

Jim was a humble, shy and polite man with a great sense of humour. His talent was beyond belief. As he became more famous he had to adapt to making speeches, doing interviews and being filmed. I feel he was never really comfortable with this.

He was a natural driver and was superb in every car he drove: from F1 to Indy cars, sports cars, saloons, rally cars and even in twin-engined Mini Mokes in off-road competitions against the army. His feel for the car was unique, and the accurate feedback he gave to Colin and us enabled the car to be adjusted to his liking. If, during a race, a problem would occur, he could adapt his driving to overcome it and continue. In one race he noticed the oil pressure was dropping on certain corners due to surge, so he would cut the ignition temporarily to save the engine, which enabled him to finish the race.

Clockwise from top:

Something seems to be baffling us.

Unmistakable

Jim in a flat cap looks on while I work away.

Trevor Taylor in his trademark yellow overalls.   *Working with Peter Arundell.*

Many times we saw him set a time in practice and then sit on the pit wall as the other competitors strove lap after lap to beat his time. If they did, he would go out and knock off another half a second, much to their dismay.

His death at Hockenheim in April, 1968 was a tremendous shock to the motor racing world. To lose his life in such a nondescript Formula Two race was such a shame. I believe he would have been the benchmark for many more years and added to his world championship tally. In my opinion, he was the greatest loss to motor sport during my lifetime, and it affected me and indeed us all for a long time.

Yorkshireman, **Trevor Taylor**, was another very talented driver with a great sense of humour. He was exceptional for Lotus in Formula Junior, winning many races before moving up to F1 as team-mate to Jim Clark. Like many of Jim's team-mates, Trevor found it difficult to match his times, but did have days when he shone. They were good friends and made a fine team. Trevor's sister, Anita, was also an accomplished saloon car racer, while his brother Mike was a very good race mechanic.

Peter Arundell was the next driver I worked with in F1. He raced with us in 1963 before becoming team-mate to Jim in 1964, after Trevor left to join BRP. A serious accident in F2 meant he was unable to complete the season. When he returned in 1966 he didn't have the potential that was there before. Unfortunately, he often said what he thought to Colin, which wasn't a wise move. He left Lotus at the end of the year and moved to America to run a computer company. Peter was a heavy smoker and we had to search him before a race to remove any cigarettes and his lighter from his race overalls, after on one occasion his lighter fell out of his overalls and became jammed under the throttle pedal!

He died in Norfolk in June 2009, ironically, on a small caravan site that we often visited, and on one occasion had seen him with his wife, Ricky. It's a small world.

Other notable drivers were **Mike Spence** in F1, **Jackie Oliver** in F2/F3 and sports cars, **Dave Walker** and **Tetsu Ikuzawa** in F3 and **Dan Gurney** during a test session in Milwaukee. I was also privileged to work with **John Miles** in several Lotus single-seaters and sports cars. And finally, **Andrew Cowan** in Formula Three with a Lotus 41 in 1966. He was better known as a very talented rally driver, and won the London to Sydney rally in 1968. He was a farming neighbour and friend of Jim Clark's. It was Jim who asked Colin to give Andrew a try in single-seaters, but it didn't suit him. I don't think he felt comfortable with circuit racing.

All the above were great drivers with outstanding individual abilities, who left a lasting impression on me.

I'm unable write about those great drivers without showing appreciation to their wives and girlfriends, who we were all grateful to for their hard work and general help. Not only did they often do all the timing and lap charts, but also collected tea and sandwiches for us all, which we would otherwise have gone without (no hospitality units then!). Jim Clark's long-term girlfriend, Sally Stokes, was always very supportive, along with Bette Hill, who was always there for Graham. Also, Gail Maggs, Pat McLaren, Jenny Parnell, Lynne Oliver and Ricky Arundell to name but a few. All were dedicated to helping their partners and the team as much as possible. They also managed to keep calm in many stressful situations, considering some were watching their partners/husbands competing regularly in a dangerous sport.

Colin's wife, Hazel, was a connoisseur at this, having been with Colin from the start and giving him full support in all that he attempted. She would complete lap charts for the team, while also trying to keep Colin from boiling over. This was a great help to us mechanics, who were all busy and could do without the wrath of an over-exuberant boss.

We were all part of the united Grand Prix circus as it was then. Whilst in competition with drivers and teams from all over the world, we managed to work in harmony most of the time and I feel fortunate to have worked under the technical genius of Colin Chapman, his designers and fellow mechanics, who continually pushed the team and cars to the forefront of motor racing. It was a privilege to have been a part of those early ground-breaking years.

Jackie at the Temporada.

John Miles
Peter Darley/JCT/CTL

Dan Gurney pictured in his F1 Brabham. I had the pleasure of working with him at Milwaukee during the secret Indy car testing.

On the grid with Jackie and his friend John Kearsey, who helped him in his early days. Peter Darley/JCT/CTL

Top left: *We were all told to 'pose' for the camera.*

Top right: *XAR11 in the car park at Wolseley Hall, Cheshunt. The venue for our reunion.*

Bottom: *A dream partnership.*

Some of the cars and drivers involved in the Jim Clark Demonstration at the Goodwood Revival meeting.

Early days at GRD with Jo Marquart.

❝*I still visit Classic Team Lotus, owned by Clive Chapman, for various events and take great pleasure in seeing all the cars I worked on in their great museum.*❞

POSTSCRIPT

My work in motor racing continued until retirement in 2010. Working as previously mentioned at GRD, then onto Modus Racing working with Chief Mechanic, Nick Jordan. Teddy Savoury was the owner, who funded the whole thing through his building company. Jo Marquart was the designer and could turn out drawings quicker than any other designer I knew.

After three years Modus ceased, and I joined Ralph Firman at Van Diemen as Development and Production Manager. I was there for 35 years, assisting over 30 Formula Ford drivers who would progress to Formula One. The most notable included: Ayrton Senna, Roland Ratzenberger, Eddie Irvine, Damon Hill, David Coulthard and Michael Schumacher.

Through the Grand Prix Trust, the organisation set up to help and support ex-F1 mechanics, I still have a chance to meet up or reminisce on Zoom with my remaining former F1 colleagues. As well as all the work they do as a charity they arrange visits to venues like the Red Bull factory, Silverstone and Brooklands.

I still visit Classic Team Lotus, owned by Clive Chapman, for various events and take great pleasure in seeing all the cars I worked on in their great museum. The first car Colin and Hazel built is there as a reminder of a brilliant man.

The Modus workshop. I'm in the foreground with John Pye and John Scott in the background working on Tony Brise's car.

The Van Diemen factory in the 1980s.

AFTERWORD
CLIVE CHAPMAN Bsc (Eng)
Managing Director Classic Team Lotus

I recognise Derek as one of the stalwarts of the Team Lotus story. He was a member of the extraordinary group of young men who enabled my father to make the most of his renowned technical, entrepreneurial and leadership skills.

Derek has done us all a favour by capturing his personal recollections of what went on. And well done for taking pictures along the way. It's fascinating to see the moments he captured and is now sharing with us, 60 years on.

The team worked incredibly hard, often non-stop. Whilst Team Lotus racing cars led the way in motorsport design they required their mechanics to work harder than any other team in order to realise their potential. And realise it they did, in spectacular style.

Team spirit is such a powerful force. To share the challenge and the triumphs with kindred spirits is the best feeling. I am sure Derek applied himself so hard for the benefit of his team mates more than himself.

Motor racing in the sixties was especially dangerous. When mechanics watched their driver heading out on track the threat of them not returning was ever present. They coped with the tragedies as a team as well. At such times, my father could not have carried on without the loyalty and support of Derek and his colleagues.

Wild About Racing is a special record of Team Lotus and motorsport in the sixties which will be appreciated and valued by any motorsport enthusiast, both old and young. Thank you, Derek, for both then and now.

THE JIM CLARK TRUST

The Jim Clark Trust is dedicated to promoting and celebrating the story of Jim Clark who won two Formula One Championships in 1963 & 1965 and the Indianapolis 500.

The charity was formed in 2015 to help support, fund and operate the new Jim Clark Motorsport Museum. The origins of the Trust date back to the original Jim Clark Memorial Room opened in 1969 by Jim's parents James and Helen and is still run by relatives of the Clark family.

The Jim Clark Café Bistro and Jim Clark Trail are operated by the Trust with profits going to charity to enhance the experience of visitors to the Museum and support tourism, culture and economic benefits in the Scottish Borders, the place Jim Clark cherished and called home. Our charitable aims focus on Heritage, Education and Inspiration.

BHP Publishing are honoured to have the involvement and support of the Trust in producing this autobiography of one of Jim Clark's former Lotus mechanics. In particular, Trustees, Doug Niven and Lawrence Johnston, who have shown great enthusiasm from the first time we approached them. Subsequently, Marion Phillips, the Trust Secretary, has been helpful throughout the project's gestation.

GRAND PRIX TRUST

For four decades the Grand Prix Trust has provided help and advice to Formula One's trackside and factory-based team personnel to put their lives back on track when things go wrong.

We also support the wider F1 community, extending to all employees (including their immediate families) who work, or have worked, for companies in the F1 supply chain for two or more years.

Our services provide effective and essential help which can take the form of financial assistance, specialist medical advice, 'signposting' to established relevant expertise and funding, and where appropriate advice relating to rights and benefits. Every case is dealt with compassionately and in total confidence.

Formula One is 74 years old and the Trust has helped members from the golden ages of Moss, Stewart, and Clark through to today. Our newly created £100,000 annual bursary fund to assist underprivileged students through motorsport colleges and into motorsport jobs is proving very effective, and elegantly closes the circle on what the Grand Prix Trust provides.

INDEX

BHP Publishing
www.bhp-publishing.co.uk

Darren and Kevin of BHP would like to express their thanks to Derek for entrusting us with his memoirs. Both Derek and his wife Shirley – they are very much a team – have been a pleasure to work with throughout the whole process. Things could not have gone any better.

To Lucy; We feel blessed to work with such a talented and thorough designer. Her ability to interpret our ideas and get it right first time is a testament to her eye for detail. We look forward to many more projects together.